The Fabian Society

The Fabian Society has played a central role for more than a century in th̶   ̶ ̶ment of political ideas and public policy on the left of centre. Analysing the key challenges facing the UK and the rest of the industrialised world in a changing society and global economy, the Society's programme aims to explore the political ideas and the policy reforms which are defining progressive politics in the 21st century.

The Society is unique among think tanks in being a democratically-constituted membership organisation. It is affiliated to the Labour Party but is editorially and organisationally independent. Through its publications, seminars and conferences, the Society provides an arena for open-minded public debate.

Oxfam GB

Oxfam GB, founded in 1942, is a development, humanitarian, and campaigning agency dedicated to finding lasting solutions to poverty and suffering around the world. Oxfam believes that every human being is entitled to a life of dignity and opportunity, and it works with others worldwide to make this become a reality.

From its base in Oxford, UK, Oxfam GB publishes and distributes a wide range of books and other resource materials for development and relief workers, researchers, campaigners, schools and colleges, and the general public, as part of its programme of advocacy, education, and communications.

Oxfam GB is a member of Oxfam International, a confederation of 12 agencies of diverse cultures and languages which share a commitment to working for an end to injustice and poverty - both in long-term development work and at times of crisis.

Fabian Society
11 Dartmouth Street
London SW1H 9BN
www.fabian-society.org.uk

Oxfam GB
274 Banbury Road
Oxford OX2 7DZ
www.oxfam.org.uk

First published November 2003

Fabian ISBN 0 7163 3059 8
Oxfam ISBN 0 85598 524 0

This report represents the views of the authors, and not the views of the
Fabian Society or of Oxfam GB, who publish it as a contribution to
research and debate. This publication may not be reproduced without
express permission of the Fabian Society and Oxfam GB.

British Library Cataloguing in Publication data.
A catalogue record for this book is available from the British Library.

Copyright © Fabian Society and Oxfam GB, 2003

Printed by Crowes complete print, Norwich

Exploding the Migration Myths

Analysis and Recommendations for the European Union, the UK and Albania

Russell King, Nicola Mai, Mirela Dalipaj

About the authors

Russell King is Professor of Geography and Co-Director of the Sussex Centre for Migration Research, University of Sussex.

Nicola Mai is Morris Ginsberg Fellow in Sociology at the London School of Economics.

Mirela Dalipaj is completing an MPhil in Migration Studies at the University of Sussex.

Acknowledgements

We are most grateful to Oxfam GB, the Fabian Society and the Dartmouth Street Trust for giving us the opportunity to conduct this research. We especially thank Pamela Young, Sandy Ruxton and Jan Penrose at Oxfam and Adrian Harvey at the Fabian Society for their continued support throughout the project. Various members of the project's Advisory Group offered helpful and constructive advice on the progress of this research; we would particularly like to acknowledge Ben Rogaly for his insightful comments on an earlier draft of the research report. The fieldwork in Albania was greatly assisted by Oxfam staff in Tirana and Shkodër. The final report was edited at the Fabian Society by Ellie Levenson.

Contents

A note on currencies

Several currencies are mentioned at various points in the text, especially in the interview quotes. Given that their use is nearly always highly context-specific, we have left them in their original form rather than translate them artificially into a standard currency such as dollars or sterling. Generally US dollars are the currency used for international tabulations and capital flows (such as aggregate remittances or per capita income comparisons). Sterling in naturally used by interviewees speaking of their earnings in the United Kingdom. And interviewees quoted Lek (the Albanian currency) for their earnings and payments in Albania. Finally, payments for travel to Italy and onward (the main migration route from Albania to the UK) were generally given in Italian Lire (since these moves were pre-Euro). At the time of going to press the approximate conversion rates for these currencies were as follows:

£1 = US$ 1.60
£1 = 190 Lek
£1 = 2,740 Lire

Executive summary and recommendations

Migration has become a central issue in mainstream political debate in Britain and across Europe. In part this new prominence is the result of domestic political factors. But it is also the result of real growth in global migration, especially the increase in the numbers of people claiming asylum over the past five years or so. Despite the higher public profile of the migration debate, the issues have become confused and mythologised. This report seeks to inform and shift this debate enabling the development of a mature, viable and just policy response.

Recent data point to an upward trend in international migration, including increasingly diverse types of movement. The total number of people living in a country other than that of their birth was 175 million in 2000, up from 105 million in 1985; most of this increase occurred in North America and Europe. Refugees, 16 million in 2000, make up just 9 per cent of the global migrant total; most of these are in developing countries, with only 3 million in developed countries. Unlike other modes of migration, the trend in global refugee numbers has been downwards for the past 10 years. Conversely, growth in undocumented migration has been particularly strong in recent years, reflecting increasingly harsh migration control regimes. Furthermore, an increasing proportion of migrants are women.

This study explores the causes and consequences of migration and considers how UK migration policy, at home and abroad, could be used to benefit both the UK and poor sending countries, as well as migrants themselves. We focus specifically on low-skilled economic migrants, the main group currently without a legal entry route to countries such as the UK. The evidence overwhelmingly suggests that the policy choice for Western governments is not between allowing or stopping migration of this kind; rather it is between regularising it or criminalising it.

The report presents an analysis of the mechanisms, trends and prospects of migration. It examines the impact of migration on individuals, families, home and host countries, with special attention paid to gender relations and to relations across the generations. Its overall aim is to provide, via a detailed case study of the experience of Albanian migrants to Britain, a framework for policy debate about migration.

The poorest country in Europe, Albania has been the European country most intensely affected by emigration over the past twelve years. It therefore suggested itself as a particularly good case-study for this task. Albanian migration has been a major instance of post-Cold War East-West migration. The exodus unfolded in a series of phases linked to critical moments in Albania's abrupt and chaotic post-communist transition, notably in 1991 and 1997. By 2000 an estimated 600,000-800,000 Albanians were living abroad, mainly in Greece and Italy, with significant and growing numbers in many other European countries, including the UK. Within Albania, emigration has been particularly intense from the northern and southern extremities of the country.

By speaking to Albanian migrants in the UK and their families and communities in Albania we were able to introduce a perspective which is too often missing from this debate – the voice of migrants themselves. Many interviewees contrasted their experiences of racism and stigmatisation in Greece and Italy with the more open-minded reaction of British society, although a few had negative experiences of racism in the UK too. However, the interviewees also spoke about how their precarious immigration status conditions their lives overall, delaying their possible full integration into British society and hindering their ability to make return visits to Albania. Few want to return to Albania for good, at least in the near future, because of the still poor economic and social conditions there.

Albanians in the UK use their migration to support their families back home by sending remittances. Amounts sent vary widely, depending on income levels and the individual's family situation. Those who are married and have nuclear families in Britain send smaller amounts than migrants who are in the UK on their own and who are supporting parents and other family members in Albania.

Fieldwork in Albania confirmed poverty as the main reason for emigration, along with inter-family vendettas and political insecurity in some cases. Many rural areas have become severely depopulated. Remittances are the key to survival for those who remain – mainly older people, plus some younger women and children. The importance of emigration as a survival strategy is reflected in the absence of young males from most rural households.

Although a few cases of 'successful return' were recorded, the likelihood of non-return was also being grasped, in most cases reluctantly, by remaining family members in Albania, along with the pain of prolonged separation. Many parents had not seen their sons and daughters for years, and some had never seen their UK-born grandchildren. For such a family-centred society, this is very hard.

Remittances, received almost always through male-dominated channels, were first and foremost used for day-to-day survival (food, clothing etc.), then to improve living conditions – indoor toilets, piped water, furniture and domestic appliances – and then for the building of a new house or house extension. Only in a few instances were remittances being invested in business activities, mostly small shops or agricultural improvements. Lack of credit facilities and infrastructure, such as reliable power, decent roads and other communications were barriers to returnees and 'residual' households initiating business ventures. Although migration and remittances were not found to be reshaping patriarchal gender relations, they were, in some cases, changing generational relationships, with decision-making on the use of the remitted capital passing from the male family elders to the migrant sons.

Our research shows that migration can, if properly facilitated and managed, have a triple beneficial effect: on the host country, particularly in terms of supplying certain types of labour which are in demand; on the migrants and their families because of the potential for improving their incomes and livelihoods; and on the country of origin through the inflow of substantial amounts of financial and (if the migrants return) human capital. However, this is hampered by several things: harsh EU and UK policies towards immigration (though there are some welcome signs of recent change); prevailing myths and stereotypes about the nature of migration and of particular migrant groups (such as the Albanians); and the difficulty of mobilising different forms of repatriated capital for the development of the home country – remittances, skills and new cultural values – because of enduring economic and infrastructural barriers.

Recommendations

The objective must be to achieve a viable and just system of managed migration, which maximises the benefits for developed and developing countries, as well as migrants themselves. To this end we propose that the EU and the UK Government should reframe their migration policies to integrate social and economic development in migrants' home countries with entry and integration in host societies. In addition we make specific recommendations for the UK Government and in relation to Albania itself.

With regard to **Albania** we recommend:

- It is extremely important that the EU, and the UK and Albanian Governments, establish consultations with migrant workers and the organisations that represent them, so that the voices of migrant workers and their families can be heard in the debates around the development of migration policy
- The European Commission should review and make changes to its Country Strategy for Albania for 2002-2006 so that it reflects Albania's development needs in the infrastructure, energy and agricultural sectors
- The EU should support the Albanian Government in developing and implementing legislation and programmes that would assist vulnerable communities to access credits and start new businesses
- International donors should direct development aid to impoverished communities in mountainous areas in northern Albania

For the **UK Government** we recommend:

- The UK should pursue a policy of managed economic migration for low-skilled workers, which creates a legal route of entry for low-skilled economic migrants.
- Entry criteria should be flexible enough to allow migrants to adjust to the prevailing labour market and social conditions within the UK, and for their personal migration projects to be realised
- The UK Government should provide low-skilled migrant workers with the opportunity to settle in the UK and integrate fully into UK life, after a reasonable period, in line with other managed migration schemes in the UK
- The UK Government should establish a comprehensive support and education system for migrants on arrival in the UK, aimed at educating migrants about the UK labour market, their legal rights and obligations as workers, advice and support on finding a job, how to access services, general social and cultural information about the UK, and English language teaching
- The UK Government should address the problem of irregular workers without legal status currently in the UK by regularising their status with permission to work for one year
- Measures to combat the informal economy should place a greater emphasis on employers who exploit migrant workers, rather than migrant workers themselves
- The UK Government should ratify the UN Convention on the Rights of Migrant Workers and their Families
- The UK Government should ensure that it sets a leading example in shifting the terms of public debate around migration, and that others - such as some parts of the media - should recognise their responsibilities in this regard

1| Introduction

M igration is a general term to describe the movement of people from their homes for a period of time longer than a visit. It can be temporary, followed by return; or permanent, with no return. Some migrations are seasonal, generally linked to temporary work. Migrations can be voluntary or forced, though often this dichotomy is blurred, as the Albanian case analysed in this report will show. Conflict, poverty, environmental degradation, food insecurity, lack of employment opportunities, and political or ethnic oppression are some common reasons for migration. Migrants range from very poor to very wealthy individuals, and they represent a diversity of skills and educational backgrounds including professionals, students, the unemployed and destitute, families and trafficked people. A further important division in the study of migration categorises migrants into two types: internal and international. Rather different frameworks and literatures have developed around these two forms of migration, but in many settings – such as Albania – internal and international movement are closely intertwined.

Since the first human settlements, there has been migration. But recent evidence suggests that international migration is increasing: indeed according to one authoritative study the current era is 'the age of migration'.[1] In particular, cross-border migration for seasonal or long-term economic purposes is a growing global phenomenon, driven above all by widening economic inequality both within and between countries, and facilitated by technological advances in transport and communications. For migrants, their families, employers and local workers in the receiving countries, migration can have different meanings and a variety of consequences. For employers and the general economy in the host country, migrants can provide a cheap and flexible source of workers, improving labour supply at both the low-skilled and highly-skilled ends of the labour market. Recently, for instance, the UK has been keen to recruit health professionals and IT specialists from abroad. However, our concern in this report is with low-skilled migrants – or, to be more accurate, with Albanian migrants who take up low-skilled positions in the UK job market.

Caught between their poverty-stricken home country and a rich destination country, these migrants exemplify the contradictions, dilemmas and injustices which lie at the heart of contemporary labour migration. Originating from a country whose exit from communism the West welcomed, their desperate economic plight, itself in part the product of neoliberal economic policies favoured by the Western powers, forces them to migrate to survive. Yet they have few legal ways to do so. Hence most can only enter the UK by illegal means or by presenting asylum claims. They are relegated to the most marginal and exploited forms of employment in which, nevertheless, they perform work which is useful to the UK economy. Despite receiving low rates of pay, the work such migrants do provides them and their families with a vital source of income which, in turn, enables them to meet their living costs. Surplus income is sent back as remittances to family members remaining in their home countries. Potentially, migration and remittances can have important effects on health, education and gender relations.

Since the 1980s, if not before, inward migration has been presented as undesirable in most advanced countries. Policies have been put in place to prevent immigration, especially from poor countries. Recently the debate has shifted somewhat. Labour shortages in key economic sectors and an ageing, low-birth population have prompted some policy-makers in the UK and the EU to encourage some economic migration. Recent reports from the UK Home Office,[2] the UK Department for International Development[3] and the European Commission[4] have presented cases for opening the doors to selected forms of labour migration, such as skilled workers in technology, health and education. In May 2003 the UK Home Secretary, following consultation with employers and trades unions, introduced expanded work-permit allocations for 10,000 low-skilled workers in each of the food-processing and hospitality industries – sectors of the UK economy where there are domestic labour shortages. Adjustments to holiday-worker schemes are under discussion as another means of easing short-term labour shortages by maximising access to young, mobile labour.[5] However, the wider debate on migration in the UK has been negatively cast, with confused and racist myths about 'floods' of 'bogus' asylum-seekers, and public discussion that is neither rational nor well-informed.[6] Alarmist rhetoric prevails, and economic migrants – whose very essence is to contribute their labour to the host country – are portrayed in the media, and by some politicians, as seeking to abuse the welfare system or as threatening the employment prospects of indigenous British workers. It is true that migrants can put extra pressure on infrastructure and public services (housing, transport, education, health etc), but overall there are many economic, social, cultural and fiscal benefits for receiving countries. Indeed the evidence increasingly suggests that migration stimulates the economy and thus the incomes and welfare of the indigenous population.[7]

These, then, are some of the general parameters, issues and concerns framing this research report. Its main concentration is on migrants who occupy low-skilled positions in the UK, focusing on the specific case of Albanians, a recently-arrived group on which there has been no previous research.[8] Albania has been chosen because of its recent experience of large-scale out-migration as a coping mechanism during the transition period since the end of the country's harsh and isolationist communist regime. Furthermore, Albania is one of several southeast European countries serving as a transit point for migrants into Western Europe. The aim of the report is to inform, and shift significantly, debates around migration to the UK. It brings to the forefront the need to ensure that inward migration does not have a negative impact on the migrant source countries, for instance by draining them of their human capital. More positively, it looks for evidence that remittances sent back by migrants function as an important means of survival and source of investment capital; and it examines the hypothesis that migrants return to their source country with enhanced skills and contacts. Throughout the investigation we examine the impacts of migration, remittances and return on gender relations and also on relations across the generations. Finally, the report focuses on the importance of increasing efforts to address the root causes of migration for developing and transforming countries, including growing inequality, lack of economic opportunity and social protection, insecurity and desperation.

The report is in four chapters. Chapter 1, in addition to presenting the background context and goals of the research in the preceding paragraphs, consists of four subsections: a brief overview of recent trends in international migration; the role of Albanian migration in the evolution of post-1990 European migration flows; a summary of UK and EU policies towards migration and the rights of migrants; and a more in-depth focus on the poverty-migration-development debate in Albania.

Chapters 2 and 3 contain the results of the field research carried out for this project, in the UK and Albania respectively. Chapter 2 concentrates on presenting and interpreting the interview data collected from 26 Albanians living and working in London and surrounding towns in the Southeast of England. It too consists of four subsections: an overview of migrant characteristics, including regional origins in Albania, means and routes of migration to the UK, and reasons for departure; a survey of migrants' work experiences in the UK; information on their access to services and levels of socio-economic integration; and preliminary perspectives on their remittance behaviour and plans for the future.

Chapter 3 examines in considerable detail the impact of emigration on households in Albania, based on 46 interviews carried out in various parts of the country. Once again, we present our findings under four headings. First we map out the different migration histories of the three main 'migration regions' of Albania. The next two subsections provide data on how remittances are received and managed, and on the impact of the remittance flows on the alleviation of poverty in Albania. Close attention is given to gender roles and to inter-generational relations in this study of remittance behaviour. The final subsection of chapter 3 looks at return migration and business development – both as yet embryonic consequences of Albanian emigration to the UK.

Chapter 4 highlights the relevance of the research findings for the policy domain. We first revisit the debate on migration, poverty reduction and development in the light of the field information collected, and then we advance some policy recommendations.

Trends in international migration

Recent data synthesised by international bodies such as the UN,[9] OECD[10] and the International Organization for Migration[11] all point to an upward trend in international migration. This upward trajectory has been established for many decades, at least since the 1960s, and some evidence suggests that the pace of international movement has quickened since the early 1990s. However not all sources give a consistent picture, and there are some countries and types of migration that buck the general trend. It also needs to be recognised that the ways of measuring migration are far from consistent, making international comparisons shaky. Furthermore, some types of migration escape the official statistics – undocumented moves, by definition, as well as some forms of temporary and seasonal migration. As the world is increasingly characterised by mobility (business travel, contract work overseas, secondments, tourism, study and training visits etc) rather than by longer-stay migration, so the statistical boundary between the two becomes more difficult to draw. Above all, international migration is distinguished by an ever-increasing diversity of types of movement: labour migrants, refugees and asylum-seekers, migration for family reunion, student migration, retirement migration, marriage migration, trafficked migrants and many more. Even labour migration breaks down into a complex typology differentiated by skill levels, length of residence in the host country, legal status and motivation. Susan Martin, writing for the IOM's World

Migration Report, sums up the categories of migratory workers:

'*At the lower end of the skills spectrum, international migrants pick fruits and vegetables, manufacture garments and other items, process meat and poultry, work as nursing home and hospital aides, clean restaurants and hotels, do gardening and construction, take care of children and the elderly, and provide myriad other services…. At the higher end of the skill spectrum, international migrants engage in equally diverse activities. They fill jobs requiring specialized skills: run multinational corporations; teach in universities; provide research and development expertise to industry and governments; and design, build and programme computers – to name only a few activities.*'[12]

With these caveats in mind, let us survey the main aggregate trends. According to the UN, in 2000 around 175 million people were living in a country other than that of their birth; this represents 3 per cent of the world population. In 1965 the figure was 75 million, rising to 84 million in 1975 and 105 million in 1985. Figures after 1989 are affected by the break-up of the Soviet Union. Leaving the USSR out of the equation, the numbers grew to 120 million in 1990 and to an estimated 150 million in 2000.[13] Including the USSR involves adding more than 26 million to the international migrant stock due to reclassification of internal migrants as international movers.[14]

Table 1 gives the size and growth of migrant stock by major world region over the period 1990-2000. In ten years the number of migrants grew by nearly 21 million, or 13.5 per cent. This growth in immigration occurred almost entirely in the developed countries of the world, especially in North America and Europe – a net growth of 13 million (48 per cent) in the former and nearly 8 million (16 per cent) in the latter. By contrast, in the less developed countries of the world, the number of international migrants fell slightly, most of this being accounted for by the 15 per cent decline in migrants from Latin America and the Caribbean.

Looking at figures for 1995-2000, the more developed countries took in 12 million migrants, an average of 2.4 million per year. Mainly from poor countries, most of these entered North America (1.4m. per year) and Europe (800,000 per year). These rates of migration represented only 3 per cent of the overall population increase of the less developed regions, but they accounted for more than half of the overall demographic growth of the more developed regions. In Europe net immigration accounted for 89 per cent of the population increase throughout the 1990s.[15]

Regarding the geographical distribution of international migrants in 2000, 60 per cent were in the developed world, 40 per cent in less-developed regions. Most of the world's migrants live in Europe (56 million), Asia (50 million) and North America (41 million). The top three countries are the United States (35 million foreign-born), the Russian Federation (13 million) and Germany (over 7 million). In the developed

Table 1 Size and growth of the stock of international migrants by major world area 1990–2000

Major world area	1990	2000	Change 1990–2000	
	('000)	('000)	('000)	per cent
World	153,956	174,781	20,825	13.5
More developed regions	81,424	104,119	22,695	27.9
Less developed regions	72,531	70,662	– 1,869	– 2.6
Least developed countries	10,992	10,458	– 534	– 4.9
Africa	16,221	16,277	56	0.3
Asia	49,956	49,781	– 175	– 0.4
Europe	48,437	56,100	7,663	15.8
Latin America and Caribbean	6,994	5,944	– 1,051	– 15.0
North America	27,597	40,844	13,248	48.0
Oceania	4,751	5,835	1,084	22.8

Source: UN: *International Migration Report 2002*. New York: UN Population Division, 2002, p. 3.

regions overall, almost one in ten persons is an international migrant; in the less-developed world, only 1 in 70. However, there are some striking deviations from this generalisation, as Table 2 shows. Not all the big immigration countries are developed: see the positions of India, Pakistan, Ivory Coast and Jordan in the top 20 list for numbers of immigrants. When the relative impact of migration is measured, the picture changes completely. Only one West European country (Switzerland) appears on a list dominated by four main groups: wealthy Middle Eastern states, newly-independent states from the former USSR, 'settler' immigration countries (Canada, Australia, New Zealand), and some West African countries. Table 2 therefore demonstrates that despite the high profile of the public and political debate about immigration in the UK and in most other West European countries, these countries are not the ones most affected by immigration over recent decades. Only Switzerland (25.1 per cent) and Luxembourg (37.3 per cent, omitted from Table 2 because of its small size) have immigrants as more than one in ten of their population.

Refugees, 16 million at the end of 2000, make up 9 per cent of the global migrant total.[16] Of these, 12 million are under the mandate of the UN High Commissioner for Refugees (UNHCR), and 4 million under the mandate of the UN Relief and Welfare Agency (UNRWA); most of the latter are displaced Palestinians. The refugee distribution is very different from that of the overall migrant population: 13 million are in developing countries and only 3 million in developed countries. The largest share of refugees is found in Asia (9 million, mainly in Western Asia) and Africa (4 million). Again, these are revealing figures in the light of the political significance and media frenzy about refugees and asylum-seekers in the UK and some other advanced countries.

Unlike total numbers of international migrants, the trend in global refugee numbers has been downwards for the past ten years. UNHCR-defined refugees[17] peaked at 18.2 million in 1993, but had fallen to 12 million by early 2001. Many factors are responsible for this decline, including the chronology and scale of refugee-generating crises in different parts of the world and the timing of return movements post-conflict, but the chief reason has been the impact of increasingly restrictive asylum policies. Following a surge in global refugee numbers in the 1980s and early 1990s, reluctance to grant asylum spread during the early and mid-1990s, when the Gulf crisis, ethnic strife in Rwanda and the disintegration of Yugoslavia produced sudden mass displacements of population. The most recent phase of the Yugoslavian movements came with the Kosovan refugee crisis of 1999, which mainly affected ethnic Albanians and also involved large-scale refugee flows into neighbouring Albania; this too has since moved into its return phase. Afghan,

Table 2 Top 20 countries with the largest stocks of migrants, in absolute and relative terms, 2000

Countries with the largest stock of migrants	'000	Countries with the highest percentage of migrants in their populations	per cent
USA	34,988	United Arab Emirates	73.8
Russian Federation	13,259	Kuwait	57.9
Germany	7,349	Jordan	39.6
Ukraine	6,947	Israel	37.4
France	6,277	Singapore	33.6
India	6,271	Oman	26.9
Canada	5,826	Estonia	26.2
Saudi Arabia	5,255	Saudi Arabia	25.8
Australia	4,705	Latvia	25.3
Pakistan	4,243	Switzerland	25.1
UK	4,029	Australia	24.6
Kazakhstan	3,028	New Zealand	22.5
Ivory Coast	2,336	Gabon	20.3
Iran	2,321	Canada	18.9
Israel	2,256	Kazakhstan	18.7
Poland	2,088	Lebanon	18.1
Jordan	1,945	Ivory Coast	14.6
United Arab Emirates	1,922	Gambia	14.2
Switzerland	1,801	Ukraine	14.0
Italy	1,634	Belarus	12.6

Source: UN: *International Migration Report 2002.* New York: UN Population Division, 2002, pp. 3–4.

Kurdish and Iraqi refugees feature prominently in figures from recent years. Quite apart from the cost, restrictions on granting asylum by many Western governments can also be seen as a response to growing anti-immigrant feelings amongst large segments of the population in developed countries. This politicisation of asylum saw acceptance rates fall to 11 per cent during 2000 and 2001.[18] Some specific trends and reactions in the UK and the EU will be mentioned in the next two subsections.

One of the most significant trends in international migration in recent years has been the growth of undocumented migration. This takes place via two main mechanisms:

- Clandestine entry, smuggled over a border
- Legal entry as a tourist or visitor, but then overstaying after the expiry of the permit or visa

Further variations on this schema include failed asylum-seekers who 'disappear' after their application has been refused, arrival at a recognised point of entry using false documents, and 'legal' labour migrants who fail to renew their permits to stay. Clearly data on the scale of undocumented or irregular migration are scarce, and only estimates can be made. Graeme Hugo maintains that, over recent years, illegal movement has been at least as large as legal migration, but this is a difficult statement to verify.[19] Most authorities concur that irregular migration has been on the rise since the mid-1970s when, particularly in Europe, policies to curtail labour migration were put in place. Increasingly restrictive admission policies have clashed with the wish of more and more people in poor countries of the world to migrate for a better life through paid work, or to flee oppression and insecurity. Another 'push' factor for irregular migration has been the relaxation of emigration/exit controls by East European countries following the end of the Cold War. Ironically the Western powers, having made political capital out of the Eastern bloc's denial of the right to emigrate prior to 1989, and having welcomed refugees from communism during the Cold War, were unwilling to accept Eastern European migrants once the migration barrier of the Iron Curtain was lifted. While this unwillingness is being modified in respect of the accession countries about to join the EU in 2004, it remains for Albania, where the desire to emigrate is widespread yet whose migrants have few options for legal migration.

An important dimension of undocumented migration is trafficking. Although the terms 'human smuggling' and 'trafficking' are often use interchangeably, there is a growing consensus that they differ. Human smuggling involves facilitating people to cross borders without coercion or abuse of the migrant; in trafficking, elements of violence, exploitation and often deception are involved, such as the trafficking of women for prostitution. In other words, but over-simplifying, smuggling is a migration issue, whereas trafficking is a human rights issue.[20] Given the large sums migrants are willing to pay to be helped to enter rich Western countries, human smuggling and trafficking constitutes a multi-billion-dollar industry. Increasingly, international criminal networks such as Chinese triads and the Italian mafia are involved, providing an entire range of services including false documents, transportation, cross-border assistance, places of residence and illegal employment – all at a high price. According to a figure which is often quoted – but again impossible to verify – approximately 500,000 persons, many of them women and children, are smuggled or trafficked into Western Europe each year.[21] Another source estimates that up to 2 million women and children are trafficked globally every year.[22] However, these estimates are based largely on speculation, and should be treated with extreme caution.

The final international migration trend we wish to draw attention to is the gender dimension of recent flows and what is often called the feminisation of migration. Many authors claim that there has been a feminisation of international flows over the past two or three decades so that women migrants are almost as numerous as men.[23] Hania Zlotnik counters this; according to her feminisation has not been a major trend, largely because migration has been feminised for some time.[24] She presents data to show that in 1965 women already made up 46.6 per cent of the global total of international migrants, increasing only slightly to 47.7 per cent by 1990. Another layer of complexity is introduced into the argument by the belief that females are over-represented in undocumented migration. This led Annie Phizacklea to claim that 'female migration has outnumbered male since 1974'.[25]

What is perhaps more important to realise is that women are increasingly migrating as independent or at least semi-independent agents – in contrast to the past when they were seen purely as the 'followers' of male 'primary' migrants. However, it is also important to recognise that women's experiences of migration often put them at risk of exploitation of many kinds. The migration of 'Third World' or East European women to work as domestic helpers in wealthy countries has been a major growth area since the 1980s. Usually these women migrate on their own or are principal wage-earners. Often they face a multiple burden, as migrants, as women, as members of a racialised minority, and because of their undocumented status.

Albania and the EU context

Despite experiencing one of the great mass emigrations of the 1990s, Albania remains practically 'invisible' in statistical surveys of global migration trends. In another sense, however, the 'Albanian exodus' has acquired an almost iconic visibility. In a thought-provoking but morally questionable advertising poster, the Italian clothing giant Benetton reproduced a picture of a dangerously overcrowded boat crammed with Albanian migrants arriving on the Italian coast. Some migration scholars have fallen into the same trap: a similar image adorns the cover of Myron Weiner's book *The Global Migration Crisis*[26]- both the picture and the title can be regarded as an inflammatory distortion of the real picture of global migration.

We can begin to get a better picture of the significance of Albanian migration if we frame it within a European context. Table 3 sets out SOPEMI/OECD data on trends in the stock of foreign population in the 15 EU countries during 1995-2000.[27] Three key patterns can be discerned from the data.

- Most EU countries saw continued growth of their foreign populations during the period under review
- This growth was particularly significant in the smaller and the more peripheral countries – Finland, Ireland, Spain, Italy, Greece.
- Although not immediately obvious from the data, the group of countries which were the main labour recruiters during the early postwar decades (France, Germany, Belgium, the Netherlands etc.) have sustained or expanded their foreign populations by other types of migration since the 1970s – family reunion, asylum migration, highly-skilled movements etc. In the southern European countries their recent immigrations, which 'took off' in the 1980s (in Greece in the early 1990s), are mainly labour migrations, although they have occurred by spontaneous (including clandestine) means rather than through the specific agreements which brought labour migrants into the northern EU countries in earlier decades

The significance of the post-1990 Albanian migration has been mainly felt in Italy and Greece, the two EU countries closest to Albania. There are no annual flow data, however, the main statistical record being 'permits to stay' (Italy) and periodic regularisations (Italy and Greece) in which irregular migrants are able to legalise their presence (subject to certain criteria) and obtain documents. The Italian data are more precise and closer to reality than the Greek figures on immigrants. In Italy, of the 1,388,153 immigrants recorded as having a permit to stay at the end of 2000, 142,066, or 10.2 per cent, were Albanians, the second largest immigrant nationality

Table 3 Foreign population in EU countries, 1995–2000

	1995 ('000)	2000 ('000)	Average annual growth (per cent)	Foreign as per cent total popn. (2000)	Data source*
Austria	724	758	0.93	9.3	R
Belgium	910	862	−1.08	8.4	R
Denmark	223	259	3.03	4.8	R
Finland	69	91	5.83	1.8	R
France (1994, 1999)	3,597	3,263	−0.97	5.6	C
Germany	7,174	7,297	0.34	8.9	R
Greece (1994, 1999)	106	238	17.69	2.3	LFS
Ireland	96	127	5.65	3.3	LFS
Italy	991	1,388	6.96	2.4	P
Luxembourg	138	165	3.59	37.3	R
Netherlands	725	668	−1.64	4.2	R
Portugal	168	208	4.33	2.1	P
Spain	500	896	12.38	2.2	P
Sweden	532	477	−2.14	5.4	R
UK	1,948	2,342	3.75	3.8	LFS

* C: Census; LFS: Labour Force Survey; P: Permits to stay; R: Population Register.
Source: SOPEMI: *Trends in International Migration 2002.* Paris: OECD, 2003, pp. 40, 294–295.

after the Moroccans (159,599, 11.5 per cent).[28] The rapid growth of the Albanian presence in recent years suggests that it may soon overtake the Moroccan.[29]

For Greece, the figures given by SOPEMI in Table 3 are probably underestimates. The results of the 1998 regularisation revealed that Albanians were by far the largest immigrant nationality in Greece, accounting for 241,561 of the 371,641 (65 per cent) who were regularised. Other important regularised groups also came from Eastern Europe – Bulgaria (25,168, 6.8 per cent), Romania (16,954, 4.6 per cent), Ukraine (9,821, 2.6 per cent) and Poland (8,631, 2.3 per cent). A second regularisation took place in 2001, with 367,860 applications; no nationality breakdowns have yet been published.[30] Although there are many unknowns – the proportion of Albanians in the second regularisation, the extent of 'double-counting' between the first and second regularisations, and the size of the group who did not apply for either scheme – it is clear that Albanians now have a very considerable presence in Greece, perhaps as high as 500,000, equivalent to 5 per cent of the Greek population.[31]

The chronology of Albanian emigration evolved during the 1990s through a series of migration waves linked to key moments of crisis in Albania. Behind the Albanian exodus, however, lay two fundamental historical facts: the considerable difference in living standards and styles between communist (and post-communist) Albania, on the one hand and West European states on the other; and the fierce denial of the possibility to emigrate throughout the 45 years of communist rule between 1945 and 1990. In this latter respect Albania was the most closed and isolated of the Eastern bloc states. Emigration was regarded as an act of treason punishable by death or lengthy imprisonment. The repressive apparatus of the ideologically-driven Marxist-Leninist regime of Enver Hoxha tightly controlled all aspects of Albanian life, persuading the country's inhabitants that they lived in a communist paradise. Unfortunately for the regime, many Albanians during the later years of communism had visual access to an alternative paradise through the clandestine watching of Italian television. Although forbidden by the regime, the secret tuning in to this Italian window on the outside world presented Albanians with a very different picture – a life of wealth, beauty, pleasure and sexiness where, it seemed, nobody had to work too hard, money was easy to come by, and everybody was 'included'.[32]

The chronology unfolded in four main episodes, as follows:

1.   The 'embassy migrants', summer 1990

During June-July 1990 around 5,000 Albanians sought refuge in Western embassies in Tirana. Eventually they were allowed to leave for the West. The Albanian authorities liberalised the issuing of passports and a small-scale exodus continued. Altogether, from the 'embassy invasion' until early 1991, some 20,000 left Albania.

2.   The main mass exodus, March and August 1991

Chaos leading up to Albania's first democratic elections (won by the Communists) led to the first 'boat-people' exodus to southern Italy in March 1991; 25,000 migrants settled in Italy. A second boat exodus took place in August, but most of the 20,000 arrivals were repatriated. The argument was advanced that whereas the 'first wave' could be treated as refugees fleeing a tense political situation, the 'second wave' arrived after democratic elections and therefore could not be given refugee status. Meanwhile a large-scale but unquantified exodus to Greece took place and clandestine migration continued to Italy. Emigration was most intense from Albania's southern villages on the border with Greece. Altogether during 1991-93 an estimated 300,000 Albanians, one in ten of the population, left the country, the vast majority to Greece and Italy.

3.   The pyramid crisis, spring 1997

Collapse of a pyramid scheme for the investment of private savings (including many emigrants' remittances) led to a period of political and economic turmoil verging on civil war in some parts of the country. This chaos produced another boat exodus to Italy in early spring 1997. Initially 10,600 Albanians were accepted by Italy, but further sea-borne migrations were turned away, sometimes in tragic circumstances.[33] As before, larger but unregistered crossings of the Greek border took place. Albanian communities already established by onward migration in other EU countries, such as France, Germany and Belgium, were augmented by new arrivals and the evolving diasporic network spread to London.

4.   Kosovo crisis, 1999

Albania played host to 500,000 ethnic-Albanian Kosovan refugees entering through northern Albania; some use Albania as a transit route to seek asylum in other countries, including the UK.

In 2000 Kosta Barjaba, the Albanian migration scholar, published estimates of the total number of Albanian emigrants living abroad in 1999, and of their distribution.[34] He estimated 800,000 emigrants, with 500,000 in Greece and 200,000 in Italy. In both these countries, the figures combined documented migrants with an estimate of undocumented migrants: in Italy documented migrants were in the majority; in Greece, until recently, most Albanians were undocumented. Other countries hosting significant numbers of Albanians include Germany (12,000), the United States (12,000), the United Kingdom (5,000), Canada (5,000), Belgium (2,500), France (2,000), Turkey (2,000), Austria (1,000) and Switzerland (1,000). Some of these latter figures are likely to be underestimates, given the mobility of Albanian migrants, especially within Europe, and the rapid evolution of new migration channels and routes.

The recent publication of the results of the 2001 Albanian census[35] has caused Barjaba's estimate of total emigration to be revised down to 600,000, although the two figures are not necessarily incompatible because they used different criteria. The 2001 census recorded a population decline since the previous census (1989) of 113,142 – from 3,182,417 to 3,069,275. But the natural dynamics of the Albanian population (excess of births over deaths over the 12-year period) would have led to an expected increase of nearly 500,000. Hence the 'net loss due to migration' statistic of 600,000. Regional tabulations in the census show this loss to be mainly concentrated in the northern and southern extremities of the country – both mountainous districts.

However the census included in its tally of resident Albanians those who were temporarily abroad for a period of less than one year. Given that there are many recent emigrants, and a lot of to-and-fro movement, especially in Greece, it is highly likely that the real 'stock' of Albanian emigrants, including absentees of less than one year, is significantly higher than 600,000. Either way, by 2001 emigration had removed one in six, possibly one in five, of the Albanian population. This is a rate of loss unparalleled in any other East European country at the time, or indeed any other country in the world.

EU and UK policies on migration and the rights of migrants

One of the paradoxes of contemporary globalisation is the relatively free mobility of capital and goods versus the restricted mobility of people and labour.[36] Migration is caught at the nexus of two opposing trends within globalisation: widening social and cultural mixing through (amongst other things) cheaper travel, rising levels of education and the spread of global culture; and deepening inequality and polarity due to (again, amongst other things) the polarisation of power over the world's economy, ideological closure, religious fundamentalism etc.

It is also worth reminding ourselves of one or two basic historical facts. The taken-for-granted way of looking at migration nowadays is from the perspective of the nation-state, yet state imposition of tight controls against immigration (and in the case of Albania during 1945-90, against emigration too) is quite recent – mainly since the mid-1970s as far as Europe is concerned. Few of our ancestors travelled or migrated under these dispensations – they were free to move.[37] This implies a narrow take on migration, whereby the overwhelming majority of the world's population are viewed as 'foreigners' (99 per cent in the case of Britain). As Nigel

Harris points out in his discussion on morality and migration, this simple reconstruction of the 'problem' of migration 'puts in perspective the awful egotism of nations [like Britain] who see themselves as the centre of the known universe'. Hence, 'discussions on immigration do not start from the interests of the world, the universal, but from those of the minority, the country'. [38]

In fact a rational, objective discussion on immigration seems impossible to achieve. In Britain, any mention of immigration trends, illegal immigrants or asylum-seekers is instantly turned by the tabloid press and many politicians into sensationalist stories of benefit-scroungers, job-snatchers and social problems. Even the current Labour Government has been at times drawn into this rhetoric, apparently playing to the tabloid gallery in its policies and public statements on the 'abusive' claims of asylum-seekers, illegal immigration and economic migrants. The negative connotation now heaped on this last term, spat out by both politicians and journalists as if such people were pariahs or criminals, is particularly significant given that the major message to emerge from an economic analysis of migration is a ringing endorsement that migration is predominantly good, for both the receiving and sending countries. [39]

Migration policies in Britain and Europe have evolved in a series of clear stages over the past 50 or so years. [40] It is as well to remember that the early postwar years were first characterised by large-scale emigrations from Europe to the New World, continuing the colonial and settler emigrations of the nineteenth and early twentieth centuries. Soon, reconstruction and economic growth led to increasing demands for labour in North-West Europe. During the 1950s, 1960s and early 1970s, these demands were met by policies encouraging the immigration of mainly unskilled and low-skilled workers from two main types of source country: former colonies in the cases of France, the UK and the Netherlands; and southern European and Mediterranean countries in the case of Germany, Switzerland and Belgium. Around 10 million immigrant workers were recruited in this way. From the host-country standpoint, there were clear differences in the way immigration was viewed: in Germany and Switzerland migrants were seen as 'guestworkers' who would fairly soon return home and hence were given few rights to settle; whereas in countries like the UK and the Netherlands immigrants from the colonies, who often held British or Dutch passports, were allowed to stay and bring in their families.

By the mid-1970s, precipitated by the 'oil crisis' of 1973/4, the conditions for the pursuit of pro-immigration policies had disappeared. As if an invisible whistle had been blown, all the main immigration countries of continental North-West Europe fell into line and implemented a halt to their labour recruitment policies by 1975.

The migrants from former colonies were turned back and the guestworker system dismantled. Some countries, such as France and Germany, set up policies and funds to facilitate return migration. The intention was to halt, and even reverse, mass migration to North-West Europe. That this did not happen was due to the strength of the momentum behind international migration, and certain international legal obligations – for instance, rights to family reunion guaranteed under European and national laws, or the responsibilities of former colonial powers towards oppressed minorities in their ex-colonies. As a result, the 'primary' migration of young, mostly male, workers gave way to various forms of 'secondary' migration – of spouses, children etc, many of whom were destined to become workers.[41] And as the structural forces driving international migration remained strong – above all 'push pressures' from the source countries – much migration became clandestine.

The UK had started measures to control immigration somewhat earlier. The 1962 and 1968 Commonwealth Immigration Acts limited the rights of entry of Commonwealth citizens to holders of work vouchers, their dependants, and the dependants of those already settled in the UK, even (after 1968) British passport-holders. These acts were passed amongst considerable controversy and racial tension stirred up by, amongst other things, Enoch Powell's notorious 'rivers of blood' speech. Primary and secondary migration continued despite these steps, even because of them. South Asians, especially, arrived, or did not return, in anticipation of the imposition of these laws. The Immigration Act of 1971 put the control of the immigration of Commonwealth citizens on essentially the same footing as the arrangements for all other foreign migrants. A new Immigration Act was passed in 1988, designed to reinforce the 1971 Act. It further tightened entry controls – for instance, by requiring migrants to establish right of abode before arrival and by allowing in only one wife in the case of polygamous marriages. Further legislation relating to asylum was passed in the 1990s and 2000s – this is briefly discussed later.

The general trend of the legal and policy framework for immigration in the UK over the past 40 years has clearly been towards greater restriction. But there are three points to be made about the British experience before we pass on to the European policy level.[42] The first is that the UK has traditionally had an island mentality when dealing with immigration – tight screening at ports of entry, and relatively few internal controls. In recent years this strategy has been severely tested, especially by foreigners arriving from continental Europe on trains and trucks, and applying for asylum, or mass arrivals at airports. The second feature of UK immigration control is its precipitation of 'beat the deadline' rushes, as noted above. The third point to recognise is that, throughout the period since the war, and for centuries earlier, Britain has generally been a net emigration country rather than an immigrant one. Only during the peak of New Commonwealth immigration during the early 1960s, in 1973 (the Ugandan Asian crisis) and for most years since 1994 (due mainly to asylum arrivals) has the UK taken in more migrants than those who departed.

For a subset of European countries, originally six, now 15, soon 25, the European Union adds a common dimension to rules and policies governing migration. Under the 1957 Treaty of Rome a citizen of one member-state is free to move to, live and work in another. This freedom of movement was seen as essential to the establishment of the 'Common Market', renamed the Single European Market in 1992. Worries over the 'southern enlargement', when Greece, Spain and Portugal joined in the 1980s, that south-north intra-EU migration would suddenly explode, were proved groundless; there was little 'migration effect' of enlargement, largely because of growing prosperity in these southern EU countries. Similar concerns over the 2004 enlargement, which brings in three small Baltic states (Estonia, Latvia, Lithuania), three small southern countries (Cyprus, Malta, Slovenia), plus four larger former Eastern bloc states (Poland, Hungary, the Czech and Slovak Republics), are now expressed less forcibly. In fact Britain has taken a lead in stating that it will waive the transition period and allow immediate labour mobility from the accession countries. This bold policy stance is founded on two points of realism. One is the belief that the vast majority of the 'new Europeans' will want to continue to live in their own countries. The second is the welcome role that a moderate flow of migrants, especially those with skills and education, will play in filling shortages in the UK labour market. It is also possible that, instead of labour mobility from the accession countries, capital mobility will substitute. This would, to some extent, repeat the experience of the past when large headquarters in the core regions of Western Europe decentralised parts of their production to the European periphery (western Ireland, Spain, Portugal, southern Italy).[43] Already, there is evidence that this is happening across the old East-West frontier.

Meanwhile, within the EU, barriers to all forms of mobility have been virtually abolished. The Schengen Agreement, signed in 1985, has led in steps to the removal of border controls within those countries making up 'Schengenland' (all EU countries bar the UK and Ireland); it became fully effective in 1995.

The melting away of internal borders has been paired with the hardening of the external frontier – what has often been called 'fortress Europe'. The fortress metaphor, however, has been somewhat exaggerated. According to Andrew Geddes, its resonance lies in its power as an idea, showing how fears about the threat of uncontrolled migration and the supposed challenge of migrants to both security and social cohesion have the effect of legitimising restrictive policies.[44] In reality the EU has neither the legal commitment nor the resources to create a literal fortress with a militarised outer border. But in saying this we do not underplay the very real threat to protection presented by those policies, grouped under the popular slogan 'fortress Europe', which seek to prevent or dissuade people in need of protection from coming to Europe or deflect them elsewhere.

Steps towards a common migration policy have been characterised by strong intentions (expressed via the Treaties of Maastricht in 1992 and Amsterdam in 1997 and in an important summit of EU heads of government at Tampere in 1999), but limited outcomes. There is as yet no coherent EU immigration policy.[45] More recently there have been renewed openings to labour migration in some member-states, including the French 'scientific visa', the German 'green card', immigration quotas for specific job sectors in Spain and Italy, and targeted recruitment of health and IT workers and agricultural labourers in the UK. The new migration scenario in Europe (and in the rest of the developed world) sees the development of an inter-national competition for skilled workers, reflecting a new economic framework that challenges previous perceptions of immigration dominated by security concerns.[46]

An increasingly important component of European immigration policies during the 1980s, and especially the 1990s and early 2000s, has been the asylum issue. The Dublin Convention of 1990 sought to establish a 'one-stop' asylum procedure within the EU, together with new forms of restriction such as the recognition of 'safe third countries' and fast-track rejection of 'manifestly unfounded' applicants. Certainly rising numbers of asylum-seekers gave cause for concern, especially in the early 1990s (see the figures for the EU as a whole and for Germany on Table 4), and in recent years for the UK, which has now become the leading EU destination for asylum-seeking. But there are different ways of looking at the figures, as the final column of Table 4 shows. Austria, Belgium, Denmark, Ireland (a recent asylum destination), the Netherlands and Sweden all have asylum ratios twice (or more) the EU average. These, together with Germany (whose ratio was higher earlier) constitute what Geddes calls the 'Euro front-runners' on asylum, prominent in calls for a common asylum policy with greater norms of 'burden sharing'.[47]

In fact, asylum rights are the most problematic EU migration policy issue. Policies across the EU have operated at two levels:

■ Firstly, to reduce the ability of asylum-seekers to access the EU via external restrictions such as visa requirements, carrier sanctions, in-country processing, and lists of 'safe countries of origin' (Britain has recently added Albania to this list)

■ Secondly, to use internal measures such as dispersal systems, accommodation centres, denial of employment, and the issuing of vouchers instead of cash-based welfare payments

Prominent NGOs such as ECRE[49] have claimed that there is a 'race to the bottom' by EU member-states that contradicts their international obligations to refugees. According to Geddes,[50] EU cooperation over immigration and asylum policy may have enabled member-states to develop new ways of regulating those forms of migration they view as 'unwanted'. EU states thus retain a symbolic, EU-authenticated commitment to granting the right of asylum, whilst eroding the actual ability of people to enter and exercise this right. However, there is evidence – above all in the increasing numbers of asylum-seekers in the late 1990s (Table 4) – that restrictions have not fulfilled their aim of reducing numbers of applicants, but have led to the growth in human smuggling and trafficking as a 'strategy of last resort'.[51]

Meanwhile the policy debate on asylum and immigration has taken new twists and turns in the UK in recent years. Table 5 provides some statistical background to the asylum debate – a quadrupling of asylum numbers between 1993 and 2002. The list of countries included in the table is based on the 15 major sources sending at least 1,000 asylum-seekers during each year 2000-02. In recent years Iraq, Afghanistan, Somalia, Sri Lanka and the Former Republic of Yugoslavia have been the key origin countries; Albania ranks 13th. The evidence of Table 5 indicates that more than 6,000 Albanians entered as asylum-seekers over the decade, but we should not discount the possibility that some Albanians are included in the figures for the Former Republic of Yugoslavia in the late 1990s (most of the FR Yugoslavia applicants were ethnic-Albanian Kosovans). Although many asylum applications from Albanians turned out to be unsuccessful, this does not mean that Albania is safe for everyone, as the interviews presented in the next chapter will make clear.

In recent years between a quarter and 40 per cent of asylum applicants have been allowed to stay in the UK, either because they are granted refugee status, or 'exceptional leave to remain' (approximately equal numbers of each). However, the 'stock' of asylum-seekers is much larger, since they remain for, typically, a year or two, whilst their application is decided and their appeal against refusal is heard. Housing and other benefits are provided to asylum applicants with no other means of support whilst they await their decisions.

The concentration of asylum-seekers in London and their alleged crowding out of scarce housing led to the Immigration and Asylum Act (IAA) of 1999, which required the Home Office to make initial decisions on asylum applications within two months, and deal with appeals within a further four months. The IAA also

Table 4 Inflows of asylum-seekers, EU countries, 1990–2002 ('000)

	1990	1991	1992	1993	1994	1995	1996	1997	1998	1999	2000	2001	2002	Ratio 2000–02*
Austria	22.8	27.3	16.2	4.7	5.1	5.9	7.0	6.7	13.8	20.1	18.3	30.1	37.1	3.5
Belgium	13.0	15.4	17.6	26.5	14.7	11.7	12.4	11.8	22.0	35.8	42.7	24.5	18.8	2.8
Denmark	5.3	4.6	13.9	14.3	6.7	5.1	5.9	5.1	5.7	6.5	12.2	12.5	5.9	2.0
Finland	2.7	2.1	3.6	2.0	0.8	0.8	0.7	1.0	1.3	3.1	3.2	1.7	3.4	0.5
France	54.8	47.4	28.9	27.6	26.0	20.4	17.4	21.4	21.8	30.8	38.7	47.3	50.8	0.8
Germany	193.1	256.1	438.2	322.6	127.2	127.9	116.4	104.4	98.7	95.3	78.5	88.3	71.1	1.0
Greece	4.1	2.7	2.0	0.8	1.3	1.4	1.6	4.4	2.6	1.5	3.1	5.5	5.7	0.5
Ireland				0.1	0.4	0.4	1.2	3.9	4.6	7.7	11.1	10.3	11.6	2.9
Italy	4.7	31.7	2.6	1.3	1.8	1.7	0.7	1.9	4.7	12.2	15.6	9.6	7.3	0.2
Luxembourg	0.1	0.2	0.1	0.2	0.2	0.2	0.3	0.4	1.6	2.9	0.6	0.7	1.0	1.8
Netherlands	21.2	21.6	20.3	35.4	52.6	29.3	22.9	34.4	45.2	39.3	43.9	32.6	18.7	2.9
Portugal	0.1	0.2	0.6	2.1	0.8	0.5	0.3	0.3	0.3	0.3	0.2	0.2	0.2	0.0
Spain	8.6	8.1	11.7	12.6	12.0	5.7	4.7	5.0	6.5	8.4	7.9	9.5	6.2	0.2
Sweden	29.4	27.4	84.0	37.6	18.6	9.0	5.8	9.6	13.0	11.2	16.3	23.5	33.0	2.7
UK	38.2	73.4	32.3	28.0	42.2	55.0	37.0	41.5	57.7	91.4	98.9	92.0	110.7	1.7
EU	397.0	511.2	672.4	516.7	300.3	263.7	226.8	240.5	288.7	366.6	391.3	388.4	381.6	1.0

* Average ratio of annual asylum-seekers per 1000 inhabitants, 2000–02.
Sources: SOPEMI: Trends in International Migration: 1999 Report. Paris: OECD, 2000, p. 233; UNHCR: Asylum Applications Lodged in Industrialized Countries: Levels and Trends. www.unhcr.ch (statistics).

Table 5 United Kingdom: inflows of asylum-seekers, 1992–2002 ('000)

15 main countries	1992	1993	1994	1995	1996	1997	1998	1999	2000	2001	2002
Iraq	0.7	0.5	0.6	0.9	1.0	1.1	1.3	1.8	7.5	6.7	14.9
Afghanistan	0.3	0.3	0.3	0.6	0.7	1.1	2.4	4.0	5.6	9.1	7.4
Somalia	1.6	1.5	1.8	3.5	1.8	2.7	4.7	7.5	5.0	6.4	6.7
China	0.3	0.2	0.4	0.8	0.8	1.9	1.9	2.6	4.0	2.4	3.7
Sri Lanka	2.1	2.0	2.4	2.1	1.3	1.8	3.5	5.1	6.4	5.5	3.2
Turkey	1.9	1.5	2.0	1.8	1.5	1.4	2.0	2.9	4.0	3.7	2.9
Iran	0.4	0.4	0.5	0.6	0.6	0.6	0.7	1.3	5.6	3.4	2.7
Pakistan	1.7	1.1	1.8	2.9	1.9	1.6	2.0	2.6	3.2	2.7	2.4
FR Yugoslavia	5.6	1.8	1.4	1.6	1.0	2.3	8.0	14.2	6.1	2.8	2.3
India	1.5	1.3	2.0	3.3	2.2	1.3	1.0	1.4	2.1	1.7	1.9
Angola	0.2	0.3	0.6	0.6	0.4	0.2	0.2	0.5	0.8	1.0	1.4
Romania	0.3	0.4	0.4	0.8	0.5	0.6	1.1	2.0	2.2	1.4	1.2
Albania	0.1	0.1	0.1	0.1	0.1	0.4	0.6	1.3	1.5	1.1	1.2
Sierra Leone	0.3	1.1	1.8	0.9	0.4	0.8	0.6	1.1	1.3	1.9	1.2
Algeria	0.2	0.3	1.0	1.9	0.7	0.7	1.3	1.4	1.6	1.1	1.1
Total	32.3	28.0	42.2	55.0	37.0	41.5	58.5	91.2	98.9	92.0	110.7

Source: SOPEMI: Trends in International Migration: 2002 Report. Paris: OECD, 2003, p. 322.

created structures to redistribute the asylum claimants around the UK, and to provide vouchers instead of cash. 'Dispersal' and 'vouchers' provoked vigorous public debate, but were nevertheless carried through.[52]

In October 2001 the Home Secretary announced a new range of measures to reform the UK immigration and asylum system. A key plank of the package is a commitment to create a coherent migration policy, with legal avenues of migration available for those with skills the UK wishes to attract. These proposals – in addition to previous measures introduced to simplify eligibility for the existing work permit system – are also reflected in the subsequent 2002 White Paper, *Secure Borders, Safe Haven*. The White Paper proposals include the introduction of a highly skilled migrant programme, changing the 'immigration rules' enshrined in the 1971 Immigration Act in order to let foreign postgraduate students switch into employment, developing the possibilities for seasonal agricultural workers, and publishing a consultative document about the working holiday-maker scheme. All these reflect the trend to 'labour market opening' mentioned earlier.

However, on the asylum front, the stance has been more restrictive, culminating in two high-profile announcements by Prime Minister Blair in the early months of 2003. The first was the objective of halving the number of asylum-seekers by September 2003. Recent publication of the figures for the first quarter of 2003 shows a remarkable 32 per cent drop over the figures for the final quarter of 2002.[53] The second proposal, to be discussed with the EU, is for the setting up of 'offshore' centres for processing asylum claims. Albania was touted as a possible location for such a centre, leading to some journalistic headlines which did little to improve the public image of that country.[54]

A move in the opposite direction would be for the UK to sign up to the 1990 UN Convention on Migrants' Rights. The Convention extends human rights to all migrant workers and their families, whatever their legal status, and seeks to play a role in eliminating exploitation. Specifically, it provides: the rights to due process; to privacy; to equality with nationals of the host country; to transfer earnings back home; to information; and to basic freedoms such as those of thought and expression. Additional rights are set out for documented migrant workers in a number of legal, political and cultural areas. Now that the 20 ratifications necessary have been achieved (as of 1 July 2003), the Convention can be adopted. Significantly, no major migrant receiving country has signed, and only one European country, Bosnia-Herzegovina.

Albanian migration: a route out of poverty and a strategy for development?

We saw from our earlier account in chapter 1 that emigration from Albania could be seen as a response to a number of features in Albanian politics, culture and economy. Above all, it was a strategy of pure economic survival for those individuals and households who had suffered most in the chaotic transition from communism and who were left bereft of income-earning opportunities and social support structures. Additionally, it could be seen as a means of self-realisation for many younger people, whose ideas and ambitions continued to be frustrated in the land of their birth; as the achievement of the long-denied right to migrate; and as a gesture of political protest against a sequence of authoritarian political figures who, in some respects, represented more a continuity than a break with the country's political past.

In this chapter we review the evidence on the effects of emigration and remittances on development and poverty alleviation. First we very briefly synthesise recent thinking on these issues at the global level, then we turn more specifically to Albania.

The traditional view saw migration as reflecting the failure of development, or worse, as contributing to a vicious cycle in which poverty is reinforced. Now, there is a growing conviction that migration can offer an important route out of poverty; migration is seen as a resource not a condemnation. The critical challenge is to understand how and under what conditions the positive impacts of migration can be enhanced, and the costs and risks reduced, especially for the poor. Hence, rather than seeking to simply control or prevent migration, or even to understand its 'root causes', the key starting-point is to accept migration as a 'given' in the global era (and indeed throughout history) and to manage it in such a way that its beneficial effects are maximised, especially for poor people in poor countries.[55] Our belief is that migration is potentially beneficial for the poor, especially at times and in places of economic and political upheaval when their livelihoods are under threat. Far better, then, to improve poor people's access to migration and to allow them to contribute their labour to countries which can use it, than leave them trapped in poverty by repressive regimes of migration prevention.

Naturally, we must guard against an over-simplistic, reductive approach. Migration, it must be realised, is a multi-scale, multi-motive process; there are many different types of migration and migrants, and the distinctions between these types are often blurred. At one extreme, migrants can be seen as responding to structural shifts in the global or regional economy (such as Eastern Europe in the 1990s); in other circumstances migration can be interpreted as a site of resistance, a creative survival strategy for the poor; in yet others it is a fast and effective route to individual prosperity, with some of that wealth being channelled back for the development of the migrant's home country.

Undoubtedly migration and development are closely interconnected, and in ways that have often been overlooked by development specialists. But the links are complex and unclear: not without reason have migration and development been termed 'the unsettled relationship'.[56] International migration and development are both dependent and independent variables of each other.[57] This leads to two questions: how is migration influenced by development; and how does migration impact on development? A third question can be added: development for whom – the host society, the sending society, or the migrant? As argued above, migration can indeed be beneficial for all. What we wish to concentrate on now are the effects on the sending society – like Albania.

The equilibrium argument posits that migration is self-correcting: as people leave from a poor, low-wage, high-unemployment economy, wages will rise as unemployment goes down. Whilst the equilibrium model may fit internal migration, it applies less well to the complex flows and structures of international migration. In fact a new consensus has emerged which maintains that, rather than stemming migration, the developmental effects of emigration can stimulate further migration by raising people's expectations and enhancing their access to the financial and cultural resources that are needed to move. Hence the 'new economics of migration' suggests that the demand for remittances, for example, increases as development proceeds and both investment opportunities and returns to investment increase; by fostering development, therefore, emigration and remittance flows propel further migration.[58] Put another way, there is a 'migration hump' that has to be overcome before people see the advantages of staying put in their homeland and migration begins to decline.[59] As we shall see, Albania has yet to get over the hump: in this country, for the time being, migration begets migration.

Leaving aside highly-skilled, professional and student migrations, and concentrating on the mass, low-skilled migration that characterises most labour migration worldwide, what are the main mechanisms that link, in a positive way, migration on the one hand, and poverty eradication and development on the other? The following are the key elements of migration, remittances, savings and return as a 'virtuous circuit'.

- Impacts on employment/unemployment. Migration reduces the pool of unemployed, either directly (the unemployed migrate) or indirectly (the employed migrate, creating vacancies for the unemployed). In addition local wages may rise, and remittances can create new jobs

- Impacts on poverty and livelihoods. Migration enables families to survive and lift themselves out of poverty – either by the migration of the whole family, or by one or a few of its members who support those left at home. Migrant earnings lead to better diet, health, life expectancies, clothing, housing, quality of life etc.[60]
- Financial impacts. Remittances have major potential developmental effects at both national and local levels. Globally remittances are estimated at $100 billion. They are a major contributor of foreign exchange to national economies, increasing national income and fuelling growth. At the local level remittances and savings can be invested in productive activities (intensifying agriculture, developing industries, setting up new service activities) and in socially useful outlets (schools, community facilities etc).[61]
- Human capital effects. Return migrants come back with enhanced human, social and cultural capital through the experiences, skills and training they have acquired abroad; in addition to their financial capital (savings), these forms of capital can be developed to the benefit of the society of origin – for instance to guide business development, foster social change, improve gender equality, reduce hierarchies of age and patriarchy, create better governance etc[62]

Of course, these mechanisms do not necessarily operate in the virtuous way proposed. There are many flip-side effects which can be damaging to the development process. It is partly the role of policy to ensure that the 'virtuous' rather than the 'vicious' effects prevail. Amongst the potential downside effects of emigration we can note:

- Loss of human capital, both qualitatively (brain drain) and quantitatively (only the inactive remain); hence local production (especially farming) and community life are pitched into decline
- Failure to capitalise on the development potential of remittances by spending on lavish consumer goods rather than on productive investment
- Migration and return lead to increased social polarisation in the home society, increasing the relative poverty of those who do not or cannot migrate
- Over-dependence on migration, leading to a remittance economy, stifling other avenues for development

As we shall shortly see, some of these negative outcomes resonate with the Albanian experience – but also some of the positive effects.

The relevance of Albania as a field-study for the exploration of the poverty-migration-development nexus can be illustrated by a few key indicators.

First, there is the scale and intensity of migration; some data and a chronology of the out-movement were given in chapter 1. Barjaba[63] characterises the 'Albanian model' of emigration as having the following features: recent (post-1990); intense (a rate of emigration much higher than any other Eastern bloc country); largely economically driven – a form of 'survival migration'; a high degree of irregularity, with many undocumented migrants; lots of to-and-fro movement, especially with Greece; and dynamic and rapidly evolving, especially as regards new destinations and routes of migration.

Already in 1995, around a quarter of Albanian families had one or more of their members involved in migration; a third of these had two or more members abroad.[64] Migrants were more likely to come from families which were larger than the national average, and generally from rural areas. These figures suggest that it was the most numerous – and thus the economically more vulnerable – families that were first affected by migration.

Second, we can note the scale of remittances, estimated at $500 million per year – higher if non-recorded transfers are included. As a result emigration has been a major factor in the financial survival of the country since 1990, and in the maintenance and improvement of the livelihood of Albania's population. A tabulation of the percentage weight of migrant remittances against exports of goods and services in 1998 places Albania firmly at the top of the list of 30 emigration countries.[65] The Albanian ratio is 154 per cent, followed by Jordan at 43 per cent, Bangladesh and Egypt 27 per cent, India 21 per cent and Morocco 20 per cent.

A third interesting indicator is provided in a European Commission discussion document on the migration-development nexus, which puts Albania (along with Mexico and Morocco) amongst those countries which lie in the 'migration band'. [66] These are countries of low-to-middle income levels (GNP per capita of around $1,500-1,800) with sustained high emigration which are at present traversing the aforementioned 'migration hump'. This means that large-scale emigration will continue for some time, but not indefinitely given the generally positive economic indicators.

Finally, we survey in more detail the nature, measurement and incidence of poverty in Albania. This provides the main causal factor for emigration and the setting against which migrants deploy their remittances and plan their return.

Poverty should be defined in culturally and historically specific terms, in order to understand the way migration responds to the perception of the deterioration of living standards, which go beyond income-based conceptualisations of poverty. According to the study on poverty in Albania commissioned by the World Bank, Albanians have a multi-dimensional view of poverty, encompassing aspects such as lack of hope; feeling excluded from social and commercial life; inability to feed, clothe and house the family; and the difficulty of continuing traditions which are seen as vital for the permanence of the family unit, such as baptisms, marriages and funerals.[67]

Before 1991, official statistics denied the existence of poverty and hidden unemployment. Nevertheless, these were present under the previous regime and were further exacerbated by the ruthless implementation of neo-liberal economic reforms in the post-communist period. In fact, the combination of the privatisation and closure of previously state-managed industries and price liberalisation left many people and organisations redundant. At the same time, high inflation and a sharp decrease in real wages reduced the overall income of Albanian households. The above factors help to explain why urban unemployment tends to be higher in cities that were industrial centres under the previous regime, such as Kukës, Elbasan and Korçë (see Figure 1, the reference map). But the general economic situation is no better in rural Albania, where the farm sector underwent a deep transformation since political and economic reforms began in late 1991. In just a few years Albania went from 600 co-operatives and 110 state agricultural enterprises to about 440,000 private farms. Moreover, productivity decreased dramatically as land was fragmented into small and dispersed lots, irrigation facilities became obsolete or were irreversibly damaged and market facilities were dismantled. Only 30 per cent of agricultural and livestock products are actually marketed. As a consequence of all these factors, agricultural production and rural living standards have fallen substantially, fuelled by unemployment and the absence of an adequate system of social protection.[68]

According to official statistics, the majority of Albania's population, 50.5 per cent, still works in agriculture, while other important employment sectors are construction and transport with 12.7 per cent, trade with 11.6 per cent, followed by industry with a mere 7.1 per cent. The registered unemployment rate was 22.7 per cent in 2001, with unemployment affecting young people in particular. Significantly, female unemployment, 28.4 per cent, is higher than male unemployment, 18.8 per cent.[69] These figures are consistent with a general contraction and involution of Albanian women's role in society at large in post-communist times. But we must not put too much faith in these statistics. There are many reasons to be cautious when referring to official employment data in Albania: for instance, all rural inhabitants who received land from privatisation are considered to be self-employed while there is no official analysis nor data about employment in the large informal sector of Albanian economy. Nor is there any official land registry.

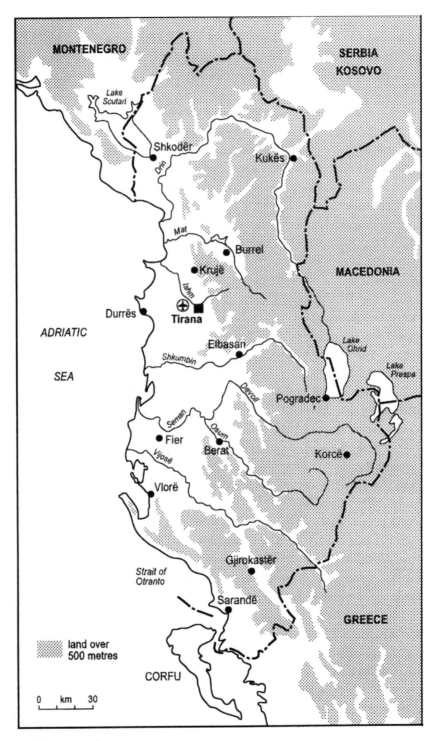

Figure 1 Albania: reference map

The 2002 Human Development Report for Albania[70] presents a wealth of comparative statistics which not only set Albania's human development index (HDI) within the global and regional (Balkan) context, but also explore geographical variations of human welfare within Albania. The HDI is a composite of three components of human development: life expectancy, education, and standard of living (GDP per capita standardised for local purchasing power). In 2001 Albania's HDI of 0.764 placed the country 70th out of the UN listing of 173 countries with data available. This was the lowest ranking of any European country. Albania's Balkan neighbours were ranked as follows: Greece 24, Slovenia 29, Bulgaria 62, Romania 63 and Macedonia 65. However, a gratifying trend had been Albania's relative improvement; it was ranked 105 in 1995. Regional tabulations show marked variations ranging between Tirana (HDI 0.822) and Kukës in the mountainous north-east (0.719).

If we refer to the parameters set by the UN-promoted Growth and Poverty Reduction Strategy, in absolute terms 46.6 per cent of Albanians are below the poverty line of $2 per capita a day, while 17.4 per cent are below the extreme poverty line of $1 per capita a day. Moreover, one in three families experiences problems with low-quality housing, while there are serious problems with potable water supply, sewage and roads, and a worrying increase in illiteracy rates.[71]

If this is true for the whole of Albania, it is also true that poverty is far more widespread in the country's remote and rural areas. Poverty indicators in rural areas, compared to those in urban areas, are nearly double at every educational level while chances of being poor are about six times higher for employed people living in the rural areas than for employed people living in the urban areas. The UNICEF map of poverty in Albania, which measures at a fine spatial mesh of Albania's communes and municipalities the incidence of poverty amongst local households, reveals the sharpness of the poverty divide between the rural, mountainous north and the interior, on the one hand, and the urbanised coast and the more prosperous rural south on the other (Figure 2). Data are often not available for peri-urban areas, where economic circumstances tend to be difficult and unstable, and where the interlocking between internal and international out-migration is most visible. As we will see from our field data (chapter 3), some of the rapidly growing peri-urban areas are even more impoverished than remote rural areas. Since these unofficial settlements around Durrës and Tirana were built by people who left rural areas, they lack infrastructure and basic social services. In most of these settlements young people have no access to education or work, and are forced to migrate in order to secure their own and their families' survival.

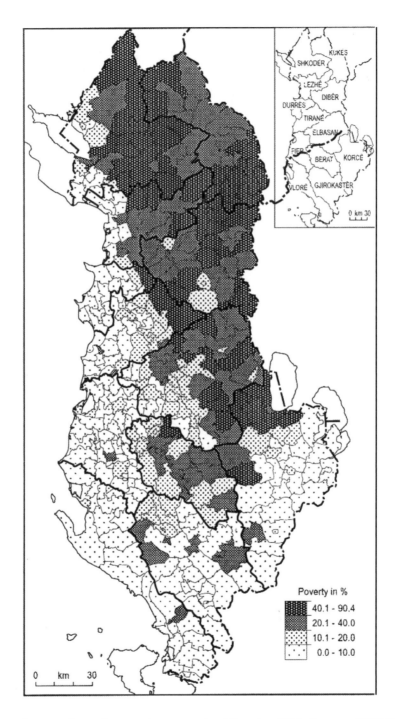

Figure 2 Regional incidence of poverty in Albania, 2000 Source: UNICEF Albania

As far as the possibility of benefiting from some form of help from the state is concerned, economic assistance, unemployment benefits and state pensions are under pressure as the number of claimants is increasing. According to official statistics, 42 per cent of Albanian households receive assistance from one or more of the above sources, the average amount per household being around $15 per month.[72] Overall the social protection scheme has a low impact on poverty alleviation and is unable to prevent social exclusion or the necessity to migrate for survival.

2| Migrants' voices: Experience of Albanian migrants in the UK

This chapter describes the experiences of Albanian migrants living and working in low-skill occupations in the UK. Drawing on interview material and other information gathered during fieldwork in London and nearby towns from October to December 2002, we provide information on the following questions:

- The place of origin of migrants within Albania, their reasons for wanting to migrate, the ways in which they are 'recruited' for migration, their means of transportation to the UK and the reasons why they choose specifically to migrate to the UK
- The skill level of the Albanian migrant workers, the types of job they hold, wage levels, experiences at work etc
- The more general social experience of migrants in the UK, including their access to social services and level of integration into local communities
- The channels used to send remittances to the home country, the frequency of contact with family members in Albania, and the attitude of migrants towards returning to their place of origin

The research results presented in this chapter are based on in-depth interviews with 26 individuals, 19 men and 7 women. This imbalance reflects the fact that most Albanian immigrant workers in Britain are men. Ages ranged from 16 to 50, with most interviewees in their 20s or early 30s. Because of the high level of suspicion exhibited by most Albanians in the UK – reflecting their vulnerability and marginal status – it proved extraordinarily difficult to persuade people to be interviewed, even more so to be taped. Many requests were refused. Interviews proceeded only when absolute confidentiality was promised. Hence we use no names, or we use pseudonyms; and no locations are given. Eight interviews were taped, while the remaining 18 were carried out by taking detailed notes during or after the interview. This affects somewhat the outcome and presentation of the research in this chapter, as the fact that most interviews could not be taped means that we often had to rely on summaries and notes of interviewees' answers, rather than directly incorporating the voices of the interviewees into the text.

Migrant profiles: origins, reasons for migration, routes to the UK

Although the small size of the sample and the role of personal contacts in the interview process do not allow us to claim that our survey is statistically representative, the majority of the people interviewed originated from northern Albania, and in particular from the areas of Kukës, Shkodër and Mat (Figure 1). Interviewees said that most Albanians in the UK came from these districts, and this distribution was also confirmed by the Albanian fieldwork, as we shall see in chapter 3. Some interviewees came from the Tirana-Durrës area in central Albania; however, again as we shall see in more detail later, most of these were internal migrants whose families had relocated from northern Albania and whose roots were in the locations already mentioned.

As far as the reasons to migrate are concerned, these vary greatly across the sample, mostly according to gender and age factors. However, most people referred to two sets of reasons: the general conditions of poverty and lack of work; and the more specific conditions of violence, political antagonism and lack of security which encompassed the events of 1997, when Albania dissolved into crisis and chaos. Here are two quotes from interviews which are typical of responses to this question. The first is from a middle-aged man, the second is from a woman in her early thirties:

I left Albania because the country was collapsing, it was straight after the 1997 pyramid crisis, criminality and political corruption were widespread. ... I just felt that my family was in danger and that I could no longer secure a future for them. I sent my first son to the UK in 1997 because my brother was already there. Then I came here as well with the rest of my family in 1998. Since I had a tourist transportation licence in Albania, it was relatively easy for me to obtain a Schengen visa for all of the family. I contacted somebody working in Belgium, paid him 3,000 US dollars and then ... we were all smuggled into a lorry heading for the UK.

We left Albanian mainly for political reasons. My husband lost his job because of the political changes. We had a private business in ****, but young people asking for money kept threatening us. The situation in Albania was dangerous and unstable in that period. The *police were also asking for money to protect you. The arms stores were open then and we were all at risk of being killed.*

People with higher levels of education also mentioned their dissatisfaction with the conservatism of Albanian society and frustration over their professional ambitions as key factors influencing their decision to migrate. Here are two extracts from young men in their late 20s:

I was fed up with my life in Albania ... everything ... the mentality of people ... the economy ... the chances offered in the professional realm ... and also what was going on at the time ... war, anarchy. ... I left in 1997. ... My family was also in need of some economic help.

You know what the situation is like in Albania ... there is no work ... and it is never safe ... but it is more the lack of work. Without money, what can you do?

Other reasons to migrate are more directly gender-sensitive. Some Albanian men, for instance, referred to the blood feuds sanctioned by kanun, northern Albania's customary law, as their main reason to migrate.

I left Albania in 2000 because lots of killings were happening in the village I used to live in. My brothers-in-law were involved in a blood feud. Insecurity and the killings are based on the kanun. Once the first killing starts ... it will never end.

Interviews with women clearly demonstrate how their mobility is heavily conditioned by hegemonic notions of masculinity and femininity, and by the pressure these exert on female life trajectories. This gendering of migration decision-making expresses itself in different ways, ranging from acquiescence to emancipation. Whereas the majority of women interviewed had moved to the UK to follow their husbands or partners, those with a higher education or coming from less patriarchal environments left partly or entirely to pursue a more free and rewarding life, including some as students. Here is a typical statement from a woman in her late twenties about the nature of 'small-town' life in northern Albania:

I left because of the Albanian mentality about women ... particularly about the way women should behave according to age. ... I mean, if a woman passes the age of marriage, which is usually 20 years of age, you will get a lot of gossip from other people about why you are not getting married and this hurts. ... Where I come from women usually marry when the are between 16 and 20 years old. ... In the small towns, when you finish school or university and you are still not engaged they look at you differently and this makes you pessimistic.

The next two brief extracts illustrate the more common role of Albanian women as 'followers' in the migration process:

My husband went to Italy and after he had been there for about six months he left for the UK. After another six months he brought us over. We decided to go only because of our children. We wanted to give them a proper education.

I left because I was engaged ... my fiancé came here because he thought that this was the place where we would stand the best chances for a better future. I waited for three years to join him.

An Albanian gay man referred to the level of stigmatisation encountered in Albanian society as the main reason why he left the country.

The main reason I decided to leave is the fact that I am gay. My family owns quite a large shop ... my economic situation was fine. I did not need to look for a job there, I used to work in my parents' shop. But the mentality there is very conservative. The place I was living in was very small and if you did anything with anybody people would find out and ... they would just humiliate you, treat you like shit. Your friends would desert you ... you would simply be alone and isolated, a terrible thing.

For most interviewees, the UK was the final destination of quite a complex migratory trajectory, which usually involved an initial period in Greece and then a passage to Italy, followed by travel overland across Europe to Britain. As the following quote illustrates, many Albanians, especially males, started their migratory careers at surprisingly young ages.

I did not come to the UK immediately. ... I first left Albania with my father for Greece when I was a kid because we had lost everything in a pyramid scheme. I mean everything, we had even sold the place and put the money into the scheme, and when it collapsed we were left with nothing. Little by little we all moved to Greece and now my family lives there. After a while I realised I could not do much in Greece and decided to leave for the UK with my cousin, he was 22 years old at the time and I was 15. My parents would never let me go, so I only told them once I had already left.

Exploding the Migration Myths

The way these migratory trips are organised and paid for varies according to the economic conditions of the family of the migrant, or the availability of strategic liaisons with the diplomatic and bureaucratic personnel granting visas. Usually, Albanian migrants do not rely on a single agency for planning their trip to the UK. People tend to arrange for a sea passage to Italy and a Schengen visa from Albania, and then draw on other contacts in Belgium or France for the crossing to the UK, which usually takes place in the back of lorries. It is usually young men who take these risky initiatives and arrange their route as events and opportunities unfold. The box opposite provides a particularly harrowing account of the circuitous route to the UK undertaken by 'Agim'. Families and single women with children tend to arrange the whole trip from Albania, travelling by plane directly to the UK or to a nearby destination. But some women and children journey overland and in the back of trucks. The following accounts illustrate these varied events and routes.

I had some contacts in Tirana and four years ago I paid 2,500 US dollars for the whole trip to the UK. … They organised the passage to Italy by speedboat, that was really horrible. I was only 16 years old. … Once I landed I was contacted by somebody and went to Milan in the back of a lorry. Once in Milan, I got onto another lorry, which got me directly to the UK. … I did not know where I was, to tell you the truth (man, early 20s).

One person accompanied us, a man from the same village I come from. We first went to Greece with a Schengen visa and then moved on to Italy by boat from there. From Italy we went to France by train and from there we took a lorry to the UK. The first time we tried, the driver caught us. He called the police who sent us to the camp in Calais. We had to go back to Paris again and found no luck there. We could only arrange to leave again on the fourth day of our stay in Paris. We did not eat or drink anything, and it was cold. We embarked in a lorry full of rubbish. There were six of us. We stopped in St. Albans. The driver reported us to the police when he noticed that we were making noise in order to attract his attention. They first washed us. Later, the police took us to the social security office. When we were sent to a hotel, I phoned my husband. We agreed on the place where we would meet up and then went to the place he was living (woman, early 30s).

I have come straight from a town in the north of Albania to the UK. I went from Vlorë to Italy by speedboat. From Italy I went to Belgium and then to the UK by lorry. Usually the driver does not know that he has Albanians in his lorry. It is very dangerous to stay in the lorry, it becomes difficult to breathe. The agents shoved us in whatever lorry came by. The driver neither knows who is hidden in the lorry, nor can hear anything. Only when we started banging and making noise, could he hear us. If the cabin of the lorry where the driver

Agim's story

In 1998 life was very insecure in Albania, I could not work nor could I save anything. Everything was a mess, the government, the roads, everything. If I owned something I would have been at risk and under pressure. And if I had nothing, then no one could help me. … I took the decision to emigrate by myself, but I was also encouraged by other people, by my friends. When I saw other people who had what I could not have. … I did not know what to expect. I did not know where I was going. But it turned out to be good.

I tried to go to Italy by speedboat from Vlorë four times. I was scared to go again in the boat after the first time I went in the water. I experienced what being in the sea is like. I was very close to dying many times. The trip was 90 per cent unsafe. It was a journey between life and death. Once we got to the Italian shore, the Italian police caught us and sent us back. They did not shoot us, though. The people escorting us on the speedboat, three people, were armed. … In the boat there were 46 men, four or five women and two children. I went by myself. In most of the cases it is men who go first and open up the way for their women to join them. In general no one had safe contacts in the destination, even if you have someone they usually let you down, they do not help you out. No one accompanied me. I was at the mercy of my own fate.

I stayed in Italy for eight months and went everywhere looking for jobs. I could not find any. I had only three choices in Italy: to be a vagabond and steal; to be lucky to have someone - impossible; to have a girl to work as a prostitute for me. Since I felt like I was wasting my time in Italy, I decided to go to Switzerland on foot. I passed by a mountain which was protected by armed people and dogs. They shot at me four times but I was lucky to escape. I walked for 12 hours without any direction, without a map and alone. I crossed into Switzerland. I got to the closest train station and I waited to be caught by the police. They did not get me although I wanted them to, so that I would not have to pay for the train. In the end, I decided to take the train to Zurich. I was with two Algerian men. We bought the tickets, but we could not understand German, so we missed the train. Then I asked a few Albanians about asking for asylum and they scared me away. I slept outside. Then I asked a taxi driver how to get to the German border. Once I got there I was registered at a camp. Although I told them the truth, they did not accept me. I was kept for 3-4 weeks. After, they sent me to the Austrian border with a letter saying that they did not accept my application. They asked me to leave Switzerland within three weeks. I was afraid I would have had to spend all my money on legal expenses so I left Switzerland within three days.

I went back to Italy. The return was very difficult. The police stopped me five times at the Italian border. I had to return back to Switzerland on the same route. I threw away all the Swiss documents in a ditch and was left without any ID. I had only some money left, about 1 million Italian lire. Once in Italy, I looked for a job and slept wherever the night found me. I slept rough for two weeks, outside. No one gave me a hand. Everyone minded their own business. All the money was gone. That was the only time in my life that made me forget about everything that had happened before. I spent three days with no food, no water, no cigarettes. I entered a village in the north of Italy, close to Milan, and I knocked on the door of a house to ask for some bread. An old lady gave me 2 kg of uncooked pasta, she did not know that I did not have a place to cook it. Then I found another lady who gave me some bread and cheese. The most difficult time in my life was when I had to beg for food. I lived almost two weeks in the fields, in old buildings that are abandoned during the winter. I ate tomato paste and drunk vinegar which were left in these buildings in order to have something in my stomach.

I looked everywhere for work but I could not find any. I did not know the language and above all I was an Albanian. There was a bad opinion about us in Italy. No one wanted to get near me because of that. I went to Brescia. I walked for five days to get there. I met some Albanians there. The first day I arrived there I went to a church, knocked on the door, and the priest let me in as my father. He fed me and gave me more food to carry with me. Myself and other Albanians ate lunch in that church for a week. Through these Albanians I could get into contact with a relative I had in England. He said to come to England. He also sent me money, 4-5 million lire, for the trip.

Every time I crossed a border I was not really scared of the police. The problem was the Albanian gangs who covered each segment. Different groups had different deals. Different groups with different prices approached me at every border crossing. I did not accept because the price was very high.

I had to go to France and pass by Ventimiglia, at the border between Italy and France. I went straight into France and neither the Italian nor the French police stopped me. I went to Cannes, where I changed train to Paris. I arrived there in the morning, about 20 hours after the beginning of the trip. I was later stopped by French police who caught me while I was trying to get through Calais. I was released once they verified that I was not under investigation. I was running out of money again and I asked the police chief the way to get to Calais. I said 'get me a taxi and send me to the port'. He laughed at me and he said 'you are crazy, how can you ask the police the way to England?' We spoke in Italian. He did not help. I took a taxi to Calais. The taxi driver told me how to escape. I was almost killed by Albanian gangs there because I did not want to pay. They said 'You have to pay because we are the gods of Calais'. They asked for 1,000 German marks. I did not have enough money. When they saw that there was no other way but to kill me, they left me alone. When it got darker I found other Albanians who had been waiting to go to the UK for months. I spent some money to buy food for them and I kept only £50 for the phone. I crept into a lorry with some whisky. That helped me not to be scared of the police. I became a bit cheerful and I started to pretend I was choosing the lorry I wanted to go on. The police probably thought I was a port worker or so. I looked at the back of the lorries. There are documents, papers which show where the lorry goes. I understood the word 'destination'. The lorry I found was carrying clothes. There was a big tube in the middle of it. I went in the tube and covered the ends with clothes. When the police came to check the lorry they did not find me. I could hear their feet above me. Then the lorry boarded the ferry. We passed Dover and drove on for another 20-30 km. The destination of the lorry was a big market. By now I was sober. It was about 1 pm. When the lorry stopped I was smoking a cigarette. The driver came to open the door and he was horrified to see me. He started shouting at me 'fucking bastard'. I said the same to him and he called the police. I was held 40 days in prison and later I was set free. I have been living in London since then.

sits is two metres away from the trailer, then he cannot hear anything. The trip is not safe at all. I paid my money at the beginning of the journey. The arrangement was that if I got caught I would return to the same person I paid the money to within three days so that he could send me again. If I returned later I'd have to pay again. It was even harder for our children – without bread, water, anything. We did not have any money. We did not know even how to make a telephone call. We did not know English. Overall, I paid 10 million Lek for four people from Italy to Belgium (man, aged 50).

When analysing Albanian migrants' reasons to migrate, and the routes they take, the choice of the UK as a country of destination seems sometimes rather casual and influenced by unforeseen circumstances, as these excerpts reveal.

Well, I am here by chance. … I did not really want to be here. I wanted to go to Canada. I wanted to be here only long enough to put together some money to go there. I was in prison for three months here ... stopped at Heathrow, for having attempted to go to Canada without the proper documents ... for nothing really. I was afraid ... they put me in the same cell with people serving a life sentence ... that was in 1996. I had come from Italy. This wasn't my first experience of emigration, I had been to Greece before (man, late 20s).

It was not my intention to come to the UK, I actually went to Italy, but then kept hearing people talking about England. ... I guess I was influenced a lot by these other people saying that 'in the UK they have a lot of money' and so I decided to go to the UK (woman, late 20s).

However, the presence of another member of the family network, or a friend or reliable acquaintance, is usually the most important element in the identification of a potential destination and the best route to get there. In addition to backing up some details on routes and means of travel given earlier, the final quote in this subsection demonstrates how this young man's entire journey across Europe was facilitated by his network of relatives in Italy, Belgium and the UK:

Nobody influenced my decision to leave Albania, I decided by myself. ... I had no future there, no job, no social life. My town was very dangerous at the time. Before coming here I went to Italy to work for one year. It is better to work in the UK than in Italy. It is nicer to live in Italy because it is a lovely place. But English people are softer and better as people. They are not so racist [against Albanians] as in Italy. In Italy they do not like Albanians at all. I went to Italy from Albania by speedboat, then I went to France and then Belgium by train. Once there, I got on a lorry and came to the UK. It was very cold in the lorry. My cousins accommodated me in Belgium. The journey [from Belgium to England] lasted three hours. I did not face any problems. I could rely on my relatives on my way through Italy, but I was alone on the trip to the UK. There were eight of us in the lorry. During the trip I heard how some people had tried up to 16 times to get to the UK by lorry. Sometimes they went on a lorry which did not go to England, or were found out by the driver. We departed from Ostend, near Brussels. When I arrived in the UK I phoned my relatives. I knew some English. I was somewhere near London. My cousin instructed me on how to take a taxi to the train station and to go to London. He helped me settle down here. He accompanied me to the Home Office and to the social security office. It was very important that I had people waiting for me here ... relatives and friends.

Work and self-improvement

By concentrating the research on low-skilled work, we inevitably encountered Albanian migrants who were in a vulnerable or provisional position – as undocumented immigrants or those who were waiting asylum decisions. 'High-class' migrants – those who were able to obtain a work permit from Albania or who had secured a good job after arrival – belong to another category of migrant. However, there is no clear correlation between educational level and job status. Many migrants with university degrees or students studying in Britain are engaged in low-paid work, for instance in restaurants and bars. Some other Albanians with poor educational qualifications had succeeded in setting up their own small businesses in the UK.

Because of their dubious legal status and their lack of knowledge of the English language, most Albanian migrants, especially at the beginning of their stay in the UK, are forced to work in the black economy; typically in the construction industry, in the catering trade and in pubs. Usually the initial period is the one in which migrants are subject to exploitative and discriminating working conditions. These typically improve once they are able to negotiate better conditions for themselves, either because they have more working experience, including perhaps a national insurance number, or because they have a better grasp of English. Relatives and friends are a good source of information when looking for a new job, but many migrants also found work through private agencies, by replying to newspaper ads, or simply by asking potential employers for work directly at their premises – building yards, restaurants etc. Here are some typical accounts of how work was first found, and then improved upon later.

When we first arrived here we didn't know anybody. There was nobody waiting for us. My brother came later on. We did not speak English. No one promised us jobs and no one offered us a hand. My husband could only find a job after we were here some months. He worked in construction. That job was badly paid, very tiring and in the black economy. He earned £25 per day for 8 hours of work. He found that job through friends. Now the situation has changed. He still works in construction but now he is well paid, £60 per day. However, he is still working 'in black' and he is paid less than his English colleagues. I have not worked here. I only attend classes as I have two small children to care for (woman, late 20s).

Well, I've always wanted to be self-employed ... but in the beginning I used to work 16 hours a day, 365 days a year including Saturdays and Sundays. I did this for the first six months. I got the first job through my cousin. In the beginning I was paid £34.50 per day. Later my boss increased it to £46.50 per day. In the next six months I started decorating houses. I got paid £65 per shift and £130 for two shifts – which means 16 hours a day. I got £195 per day when I worked three shifts – all the time basically. I had to work more because I had economic obligations. All this has lasted for about 16-17 months. After that I made some progress with the language and I started to work privately. I worked as a painter and decorator, doing floors, woodwork etc. This is how I opened my own small refurbishment firm. I started my own business a year after my arrival (man, early 30s).

In the beginning it was very difficult to find a job for myself or my husband. We did not have a network and we did not know the language. At that time it was very difficult for Albanians to find a job. I have been unemployed for over a year and a half. During all this time I have studied the language. To find a job is more difficult for a woman than for men; usually Albanian women work in hotels, cooking, cleaning. The ones I know contacted some hotels in central London and started working off the books. They usually earn £120 a week and work eight hours a day. They are paid under the minimum level of payment, without a contract and in cash (woman, early 30s).

Most Albanian migrants are employed in manual and low-skilled jobs. Over time some improvements in pay, conditions and status may be achieved. As illustrated in the excerpts above, men usually work in the construction sector with some working in pubs or restaurants. Women, if they work at all, tend to work in shops, restaurants, or as cleaners and other manual occupations in hotels or for private houses. The level of payment is usually at or below the minimum wage. Here are some more examples which reinforce this general picture and give insights into relations at work. The last of these extracts gives some hints about gender relations within Albanian households in the UK:

I worked in a bread factory, as a customer service operator, in a clothes shop, in construction. … In the most recent job I have been working for two months. There are few opportunities for longer-term jobs. Generally we can get jobs up to six months. I wanted to move from those jobs because I was not happy with them …. they are boring and time never passes. … I want to have a job that enables me to have a good time and to learn something as well (man, early 20s).

My husband found his current job through a friend. He has a contract now and I think it is quite a regular job. From what he tells me there is no discrimination where he works, however I know that in other places where my cousins work Albanians are paid less and they do not have a contract. My husband is paid weekly up to £350. He is satisfied with his wages (woman, mid 20s).

He found the jobs himself. We went around asking in the neighbourhood. In other cases he found a job through employment agencies. But his friends are always the ones who give him advice and help him out with work. I think right now he is satisfied with his current job. His colleagues are English and he did not tell me about any particular problem at work ... but other English employers were very racist in regards to foreigners. Once he was involved in a fight with a black colleague ... but he does not like talking about these things. ... I think he has a contract now ... his employers asked him for documents, language, insurance number, etc. All his friends work in construction because their asylum applications were refused. Employers usually do not ask for an insurance number in the construction business (woman, mid 40s).

Access to social services and levels of integration and discrimination

Interviewees who had come to this country seeking asylum were initially provided with accommodation by social services and were registered with the local education and health services, which they all indicated having regular and unproblematic access to. Although asylum-seekers can receive accommodation and support for as long as their asylum claim is under consideration, in many cases they decided to quit these supports, take jobs and live on their own devices. This 22-year old woman from northern Albania was a good example of this strategy:

Well, when I first got here I became a refugee with no documents. ... I still haven't got them, but I have applied at the Home Office. ... I hope to improve my situation somehow by showing that I do not intend to take advantage of the subsidy system. For instance, as soon as I could I stopped claiming benefits, I started going to school. ... I think that if you ... prove that you are no trouble-maker ... all of these things might help you obtain documents.

This report makes no judgements on the strength or justification of these people's claim for asylum: some had received a positive decision from the Home Office, some had been refused, and others were still awaiting an outcome. However, whatever their need for international protection, the survival of the family unit back home remains an important motivating factor. Younger men send most of their income back to Albania, as this young refugee with Exceptional Leave to Remain illustrates:

Yes, I got documents, until 2005 ... but I had other problems ... they caught me working and told me, either you work or receive assistance. ... Then another problem is that they wanted to move me north, out of London. I refused both to give up my job and to be moved away from London and decided to leave the accommodation they had arranged for me and live without any kind of support. For one and a half years I paid everything myself, I was less than 16 years old. While I was receiving benefits I could send a lot of money home, as I

Besnik's story

Like many other Albanians hoping for a better life, I went to Greece in 1995 for the first time, when I was 15 years old. I managed to pass through the border near the Kapshtica checkpoint. I walked 200 km in four days. We had to walk during the night to avoid Greek police or army patrols. In the end I arrived in the town of Veria (northern Greece). I hardly managed to find work as I was only 15 years old at the time. I even started smoking in order to look older. During the summer I worked for three months picking peaches, earning 2,500 drachma per day, sometimes 3,000, including lunch. This was the longest I had ever been away from home, so I returned home in October.

In March I was back in Greece illegally to find work. This time we couldn't complete our journey deeper into Greece because a friend of ours broke his ankle and we all had to go back to Albania. We gave ourselves up to the Greek military, who happened to be driving in a country road near where we were. They took us in the back of their truck to their barracks. When we arrived there we were given a welcome beating up. I was dragged by my hair and the soldier said in Greek 'where do you think you are going with your long hair?' I asked another soldier in English what I had done and why I was subject to such treatment and he said that he was a new soldier, that the others wouldn't listen to him and that he couldn't do anything. Later that afternoon we were ordered to cut wood and to clean the military barracks. We cleaned the dining room where about seven soldiers were having their lunch and watching porn movies on the television set installed high on the wall at the end of the big room. When we had finished the soldier in charge took me by my hair and invited all the other soldiers to see how they were going to cut my hair. They sat me in a small room, which I think was the barber's room and had a laugh wondering how I would look like after they had cut my hair. One of them approached me with scissors and for a moment I felt powerless. Sometimes you don't believe that a situation is actually taking place at first and I realised they were serious only after a while. I then started shouting and threatened to hit my head against the wall if they were going to come near me and touch my hair. I think they were frightened and pretended to be joking. The soldier in charge who had called on everyone to see the 'show' took me back where the other Albanians were, in an underground tunnel which was full of water up to the knee and gave me a kick in the stomach, saying that it was for the way I had offended him in front of the other soldiers by not accepting to have the haircut. I was determined not to have the haircut and I said to myself that hardly anyone had died of beatings.

Later that day we were packed on the back of a truck, about 30 of us, and taken to the border point at the customs house. These crazy stories have no end and I would go on for hours if I were to mention them all. We have been subject to very bad treatment, from local Greek or Italian authorities. The political circles of these countries turn a blind eye to these violations of human rights. Perhaps the most ironic consideration is that these countries are members of the European Union and have still got so much to improve on their human rights records, and soon they will have the lead in the European Community. Recently there were demonstrations in Rome from Albanians in Italy saying 'enough with racism', 'enough with chauvinism'. We are tired of this treatment from our Greek and Italian neighbours and now we see we aren't guilty of anything. The criminal thugs that operate in these countries have nothing to do with those working hard to earn a living and I think the law should deal with them accordingly.

When I arrived in Britain, I entered illegally just like in Greece and was offered shelter and education. I don't see Britain as a soft touch country but as a civilised country giving an opportunity to those in need of help. I attended a two-year course in Information Technology and obtained qualifications in English, Spanish and Italian languages. Who would have thought that this young man in Greece, who had been looking for any kind of job in Greece, would have fared so well in Britain in only a few years time?

saved on housing expenses. Later I also saved a lot of money on housing as I used to share a room with six other young people … we were working in shifts so we did not need to be indoors at the same time. I used to be a waiter and paid my food and accommodation with tips, the rest I would send home.

During the late 1990s the UK emerged as one of the favourite destinations for Albanian migrants - it came to be considered as a country where Albanians could start a 'new' life, away from the repressive stigmatisation and criminalisation they had encountered in Italy or Greece, the two main destination countries for Albanian migrants since 1990. Most interviewees spontaneously indicated the lack of racism in general, and of a 'bad reputation' for Albanian migrants, as positive features of their experience in the UK. In the above box we read the story of Besnik, who had been badly abused by the authorities in Greece but had subsequently found a much more welcoming sanctuary in Britain. However, when talking to some of the interviewees, experiences of discrimination and antagonism at work and at school were actually not so rare, with the media clearly implicated in shaping attitudes.

When we used to watch television with my English family ... it was really embarrassing sometimes when they talked about the Albanians. ... Do you know what my landlady told me? She told me that if I had told her on the telephone I was Albanian she would not have accepted me in her place (man, early 20s).

Well, there are problems with English people. ... They have a bad opinion of Albanians. They think we are capable of anything. ... Well, if they listen to the newspapers and the news, of course ... I can't blame them. Normally employers do not really mind and just want the job to be done ... but English colleagues can be very racist. I remember somebody used to call me 'you Albanian refugee'. When you start a new job, if you are a bit chatty they think you are a fool and say 'you Albanians are capable of anything' (man, early 20s).

Sometimes I feel discriminated. ... I mean, everyone is friendly when they chat to me ... until they know I am Albanian. When I say I am Albanian they usually interrupt the conversation and find an excuse to leave. Why does this happen? Is it because we are refugees? Or is it because we brought crime? If you read the newspapers you'd think that Albanians are the only ones behaving badly. ... They humiliate us...they just do it on purpose, only to discriminate Albanians. I know there are Albanians who make trouble, but not everyone is the same. The public opinion kills me in the UK (woman, mid 20s).

From the very first days I came here I was sent to a girls' school. I was 14 years old. I did not know English at all. I had to go through a very difficult period. Other girls were giving me a hard time, English, Indians, Black Caribbean. They were jealous and hated me. They did not accept me when working in groups. ... There is a lot of discrimination going on at school. Teachers know the situation in Albania and take the piss out of us ... they say in front of everyone in the class that everything bad in Europe is done by Albanians. ... 'You are all criminals ... you hold the drug in one hand and the gun in the other' ... this kind of thing (girl, teenager, still at school).

Nearly all interviewees denied having experienced discrimination or unfair treatment in relation to access to social and health services. However, there were one or two significant exceptions, as this excerpt from a woman asylum-seeker indicates.

I had lots of problems with the social security office. They always ask me to bring my children along. They make me wait for hours before they see me ... overall I think they are very racist. I feel as if they have assaulted me and harassed me emotionally time after time. For instance, they did not believe me when I was in hospital with my son. That lady made me cry many times in front of her in the social security office. I also had a few problems with my accommodation. I lived in a single hotel room for nine months, it was two metres by three ... can you imagine? I was with a child and pregnant at the same time. Only two months before my delivery time did social security give me appropriate accommodation.

Overall, most of the interviewees declared themselves satisfied with their experience of migration to the UK. Lack of documentation and legal status was indicated as their main disappointment and problem. Albanian migrants' precarious immigration status conditions their experience of emigration all round, by hampering their access to regular jobs and better working conditions, denying them the possibility to return home to visit their families, and ultimately by keeping their migratory projects indeterminately on hold. This latter factor plays a key role in remittance behaviour, as we shall see presently. In brief, it prevents Albanian families from investing in and planning their future life trajectories, whether these be in the UK or in Albania. However, most interviewees said that if they had the choice they would rather stay in the UK and return to Albania for their summer holidays and family visits. When asked what would have to change in Albania in order for them to want to go back and live there, most interviewees simply answered: everything. The lack of a genuinely democratic political culture, of basic infrastructures and employment opportunities, together with enduring poverty and tough living conditions were identified by most interviewees as the main obstacles preventing them from returning to Albania. The following interview quotes and summaries flesh out these points.

Well, my status hasn't changed and I still don't know how long I am entitled to stay in this country. ... I would love to get the documents so that I could go and see my parents. ... I mean, now I am paying taxes, my own rent, everything, just like an English person ... the only difference is my documents, I mean, I don't want a temporary permit to work, I want proper papers, to come and go when I want. I would really like to invest here, more than I have done so far. But I don't know how long I will be able to stay here. ... If I knew, I would invest more money here ... or there, but to tell you the truth my parents keep telling me that the situation is worse than when I left. ... I don't want to return ... for me to return everything would have to change: politics, the government, the economy, roads, electricity, water (man, mid 20s).

Well, I imagine my future here, I am not going to move from here. Only if they send me back, I will go to my place of birth. If they give me the right to remain I will go to Albania only for a short period. I might consider returning to Albania only if there is a strong government, able to guarantee security, maybe then I would return (man, early 40s).

If only I had the money I would invest everything I have here ... for my own future, but most of all for the future of my new family here and the well-being of my family back in Albania. ... What would have to change in order for me to return to Albania? Everything, from water to electricity, the government ... I mean, everything (woman, early 20s).

Remittance behaviour and gender roles

Most Albanians help their families at home by remitting a considerable part of their wages. Further detailed consideration of the use and deployment of these remittances will be given in our account of the Albanian field surveys in the next chapter of this report. Given the structure of the report, reflecting fieldwork in two countries and the importance of remittances in the migration-development relationship, we separate the host-country perspective on remittances from the home-country setting. We also pay attention in this subsection to the gender dimensions of migration and remittances.

Usually remittances are higher in the first years in the UK, when the need to improve living conditions back home is most urgent. The amounts sent vary according to the needs of the households at home and to the economic situation of the migrants in the UK. Whenever the migrant lives with his/her family in the UK, the amount of money sent to Albania decreases considerably, since the focus switches to achieving better conditions for the family unit in the emigration context. In general, single men, young people and those whose life trajectory is still anchored at home are the ones who send the largest amounts. These on average range between £2,000 and £10,000 per year. However, larger family units have been able to save and send home £10,000-£30,000 a year or more. This usually happens when two, three or four people from the same extended family pool their resources. Since only a few Albanian migrants have been able to regularise their position in the UK, and thereby become able to move freely between the UK and Albania, the most usual way to send remittances home is through Western Union. This is a direct consequence of the precarious status of Albanian migrants in the UK. Usually money is kept in a bank account in the UK and then sent to the family unit at home when need arises. In the majority of the cases money was not sent regularly, but two or three times a year.

Some interviewees save money to guarantee better living and working conditions for themselves and their families in case they are forced to return to Albania. The ideal plan is that their savings will enable them to buy or build a new house and/or start a new economic activity, usually related to the experience achieved in the context of emigration. Others, especially those whose migration project has already formed around the idea of returning to Albania, are busy investing their remittances in the construction of a better home in Albania. This is seen as a safe and flexible investment for Albanians working abroad as it enables them to improve their parents' and relatives' living conditions while securing at the same time a better house to live in for themselves in case of repatriation. Here are some typical cases of remittance behaviour. In these quotes and the ones that follow in this section, all interviewees originate from northern or north-central Albania.

I supported my family in Albania for the first two years. I sent them up to £4,000 a year. With this money my family bought some land to build a new place and bought new furniture. I think a lot about them and I am ready to help them any time they need money. But I am very careful about the way they are going to spend it. I want to know what the money is needed for and I usually tell them how to spend it. I will continue my business here if I will still be living in England. If I am sent back, I will save up in order to invest in Tirana. I want to open my own construction company as I am skilled and ready to continue working in this sector. I have sent to Albania a total of £50,000 as a result of four years of work in the UK (man, early 30s).

We have supported both of our families, although slightly more my husband's. The money was used to build the new house and to buy new furniture. My husband is paying monthly for the education of his brother. He is also sending money to his sister who is completing a university degree. However ... they are never content with what we send ... they always ask for more. They think that it is easy to make money here. We sent a lot in the beginning, up to £2,500 per year, but not any longer. Sometimes I argue with my husband because he always agrees to give them money ... and they decide how to use it as well ... all they do is ask my husband for money and he gives it to them (woman, mid 20s).

You know how it is where I come from ... once you marry you become part of another family ... you cannot really help your family [of origin] any more. ... I might send a present to my mother every now and then, so that she can buy something special for herself, but the rest of the money I get is for my own family here and my husband's at home. We put the money in the same account and then he sends some home whenever they ask for it (woman, early 20s).

Yes, I help my family at home, I send them money so that they don't have to worry about anything. I do not keep my money here, because it is not safe. Anything can happen. I do not use banks. I mainly use cash. I keep my money safe here. I don't care what they use it for. The most important thing is that my family is OK. So, every two months I send about

£2,000. If I have to return I will definitely buy a house in Tirana. Otherwise I will go to Albania only for holidays (man, early 20s).

I have helped my family in Albania. We have helped the brothers and sisters from both sides. Every time they have problems they give us a ring and then we call them back. When this happens they always ask for money. My husband has sent money to his two brothers. He sent 2 million Lek to one of them because he wanted to buy a car, and 4 million Lek to the other one because he needed to buy some material for his business. He also sent money to his sister, so that she could buy some land to build a new house in Tirana. I sent money home too, 5 million Lek to my brother who wanted to buy a new house in Durrës. My husband has bought some land in Tirana. He thinks either to build a house or to buy a flat in Tirana. We send the money via Western Union ... my husband does everything ... he keeps all the money in his name, in his bank account. No one else has access to it. He still takes decisions as it was before in Albania (woman, 40s).

Understanding the way remittances are both sent and spent - with the help of these and other testimonies - enabled us to uncover some interesting gender-power and generational dynamics shaping the migratory project both at home and abroad. According to Albanian custom, when a daughter marries, she leaves her household of origin and becomes an integral part of her husband's household. This means that theoretically a married woman has no economic responsibility towards her parents, but only towards her husband's family. This has important implications for migrant couples' remittance behaviour as usually it is sons who remit to their parents. Daughters are only allowed to help their parents or relatives in special and exceptional occasions. Usually this takes the form of small amounts of money considered as a kind of 'special present'; at the same time, they are expected to contribute regularly to their parents-in-law's well-being. In the majority of the cases, as illustrated above, it is the husband who administers the financial resources of the household and manages the remittances. Typically the money is sent to the male head of the family at home, who then deploys it on behalf of the whole family. As we will show in more detail later, the economic power achieved by the migrant abroad usually means that he has the possibility to negotiate with the head of the family at home the way his own money is spent. The following interview extract illustrates a case where some generational power shift in favour of the migrant son is suggested; but gender relations appear more immutable. The interviewee is a young man aged 22 from northern Albania.

My father is the one who decides everything ... but now he listens to me a lot more. Now, if I don't agree with something he usually respects what I say.

MD: Is it because it is your money now?

Well, look, we don't put it that way ... this is the money of the family and my father is simply the head of the family.

MD: Does your mother have a say? Can she disagree with the way money is spent?

Well, it has never happened ... if my brother or my father decide something ... I mean they would not decide something if somebody in the family would disagree ... if they decide to build a new house they do so for the whole of the family ... not just for themselves.

MD: What about your wife, can she disagree?

It doesn't make any difference, I mean, she is still part of the same family.

MD: But what about the place you might go back to live in, in Albania ... maybe she would rather live alone with you in a different place than with your parents?

No, no. She knows very well what our economic conditions are.

Several of the previous interview clips also allude to another important aspect of the Albanian migratory process - the way in which emigration to the UK is inter-woven with internal migration within Albania. As noted earlier, most Albanians in the UK, especially those involved in the low-skilled end of the labour market, orig-inate from northern Albania; but some families from this area had already relocated internally to the main towns of central Albania before some family members emigrated. In a number of the extracts given above it is clear that, even for those who migrated direct from the north, the intention upon return is to settle in the Tirana area. If they have to return to Albania, this is where they see their future. Hence emigration to the UK (and presumably to other countries) functions as a mechanism of inter-regional, generally rural-urban, migration within Albania.

Although emigration has offered Albanian women and men the possibility to experience themselves in new ways, most migrants, especially those from northern Albania, seem to reproduce the same canons of masculine and feminine roles and behaviour they brought from home. However, young women seem to be more critical of the level of submission Albanian women are subject to according to Albanian customs, and find comfort in the friendship of their English friends and colleagues. The question asking interviewees if they ever had a relationship with a non-Albanian partner was the one around which the contrasting attitudes and experiences of Albanian men and women in relation to tradition and cultural change emerged most clearly. The following interview quotes, necessarily long, illustrate some of these contrasts and tensions.

My family continues to control me. My older brother controls me, he interferes in everything. He is over-protective and won't allow me to have a boyfriend. He gets in my way even more than my father does. There are lots of Albanian men here and very few Albanian girls, who came with their families. They usually spend their time selling themselves as pure and playing the role of virgins in order to show Albanian guys that they are good. Because Albanian men want you to be pure, to be a virgin. Our families keep us closed in at home, under surveillance, because they are afraid of gossip. All Albanians here came from the North and everybody knows everybody. An Albanian guy threatened to marry me ... and now my parents want to force me to marry him. I don't want an Albanian man, because he does not care about you. He goes straight to his thing and thinks only about his own pleasure. He has got no sexual experience ... on the contrary English boys do some foreplay, they tell you sweet words, I mean, they know how to do it. ... I had an English boyfriend once ... it was completely different from an Albanian guy. I hate Albanians. All my friends are foreign, not Albanian. Every time I walk out on the streets Albanian men look at me and talk dirty to me. My English boyfriend never asked me to do things I would not fancy, while an Albanian man wants to marry you only to do the housework and to fuck you every night. My family wants me to marry an Albanian man, because they are fanatical, they think English men do not respect you because they do not want to marry you. They want to go back to Albania one day, but I don't, I want to stay here and go to college, to enjoy myself. They do not understand me. I do not want to marry now. I want to be independent. I want to choose the one my heart wants. I want to go away from these fanatics. We are not in Albania (teenager).

Albanian women don't get to know that many people here because it is very difficult for them to go out ... you know the Albanian mentality goes on here as well. They have kids, they must take care of the place ... there are very few possibilities for them to be free. My situation is different ... for women like me it has changed a little bit ... with my husband we understand each other, but in the end it is him who decides ... the money we make we put it together, in the same account, and if I need something I have to ask him. He never says no, but I still have to ask him. My money goes straight into his account, just like in Albania, only the technology changes. … But I would not want to have a foreign partner, it would be against my values, because it is known that an Albanian man would never leave you, while foreign men can do what they want. … I think these English girls are too free, they spend their nights at the pub, I mean every night. … I understand that they might want to go to the pub sometimes, but not always. It is not a place for women. And when they go out they do not ask permission of their parents, they just do what they want and don't think about what the neighbours might think (woman, early 20s).

Yes, I have been with English and Spanish girls. English women do not like men to take control over them. They want to be independent, to see the guys occasionally, to phone them up every now and then. We have to accept that, otherwise they will say 'see you later'. I prefer Western European women to tell you the truth, because Eastern European women are just after your pocket. I have never been with an Albanian partner in the UK, because there are not too many Albanian women around (man, early 20s).

Yes, I had foreign girlfriends … mainly Spanish but also English, Polish, Russian. … I do not have any problems. The main problem Albanian men have with foreign women is that after a while they want to leave, but Albanian men cannot accept that and try to keep them by all means. I cannot stay with a foreign woman for a long time. … However, I haven't been with an Albanian woman for a while. Indeed I do not know them at all. Maybe I would prefer to be with an Albanian woman because of the language and because they are different from foreign women, I think they are more stable and mature. It depends also on the man. If the man is smart and strong the Albanian woman will be even better. I mean, there is no one like an Albanian woman, she listens to you, while the English woman will simply tell you she is going to the pub, whether you like it or not. … [But] … it is difficult to meet up with an Albanian woman ... they are kept like in a prison, as if they were living in Alcatraz … they are always controlled by their families (man, early 20s).

As far as leisure and free time are concerned, Albanian migrants' mobility and participation in social and cultural life are very much shaped by their gender, as the interview extracts above clearly show. Most Albanian women find in emigration similar conditions of oppression and submission to those they encounter at home, but many younger Albanian men and women seem to be open to experimenting with different moral trajectories. Interestingly, these often match with alternative and less homebound migratory projects.

3| Back home: The impact of migration on households in Albania

I
n this chapter we analyse the ways in which the effects of emigration – and in particular the remittances sent by Albanian migrants living and working in the UK – impact on the social, economic and cultural development of poor or previously poor migrant households in Albania. As elsewhere in our analysis, we pay particular attention to gender dynamics and cross-generational change. We first outline the regional dimension. This is important, since we need to explain why the sample of households we interviewed can be seen as representative of regional contrasts in patterns of Albanian migration. Three regional migration systems were identified, broadly corresponding to the predominantly rural north of the country, the predominantly rural south, and the more urbanised central and coastal regions. The remaining three subsections focus on remittances and return. More specifically, they address respectively the following three sets of questions:

- The member of the household who receives remittances and the mechanism used to determine which household member is responsible for making decisions about the distribution and use of remittances
- The uses to which the remittances are put within and outside of the household, including the impact of remittances on household income and poverty levels
- The extent to which returning migrants are able to reintegrate into the community and establish livelihoods for themselves

We address these issues by drawing mainly on ethnographic and interview material gathered during fieldwork in Albania between December 2002 and February 2003. We also draw on previous visits and general knowledge of the Albanian migration scene, and on published literature and statistics.

We collected 46 interviews during the Albanian fieldwork, most of them taped and subsequently transcribed and translated. Of these, eight were 'key-informant' interviews with officials and representatives of UNHCR, IOM, the Albanian Ministry of Labour and Social Affairs, the Ministry of Public Order, local NGOs etc; many of these interviews took place in Tirana. The remainder of the interviews were with families, households and individuals who had close relatives (typically sons or daughters) living in the UK or, in a few cases, with returnees from the UK. These migrant and migrant-household interviews were distributed as follows: 12 in northern Albania, in the areas around Shkodër and Burrel; 22 in the peri-urban districts outside Tirana and Durrës in central Albania; and four in the south, in Lushnjë and Vlorë. This uneven distribution broadly reflects the geography of Albanian migration to Britain, with its origins primarily in northern Albania, and the parallel process of intense internal migration to Tirana and Durrës from the north.

In selecting the sample to be interviewed we tried as much as possible to interview an equal number of men and women. However, given the conservative nature of northern Albanian society, more often than not it was impossible to interview women away from the rest of the family. In fact, in nearly all cases, interviews conducted in these areas were family interviews, with the male head speaking on behalf of the family group. However, usually the interviewing context was extremely friendly and relaxed, and the fact that the issues raised during the interview were not seen as particularly controversial – unlike the interviews in the UK – meant that everyone, including women and children, felt relatively free to express their own ideas quite spontaneously.

At the time we carried out the interviews Albanian potential migrants were in a difficult situation: their enduring necessity to migrate in order to guarantee the economic survival of their households clashed with the Albanian state's success in curbing illegal emigration into Greece and Italy. Since the end of 2002, traditional emigration channels such as the sea passage between Vlorë and Otranto (on the Italian coast), and the many mountain routes on the Greek-Albanian border, were blocked, resulting in heightened corruption practices; the cost of a 'fake' Italian or Greek Schengen visa soared to around 2,000 Euro. These costs can be seen as increasing the vulnerability of Albanian migrants, many of whom are forced to stay longer in the country of destination in order to pay back the amount which was necessary to exit Albania. This is particularly true for those who have to resort to borrowing money from local power-brokers, as these can retaliate against the members of the family household remaining at home.

Exploding the Migration Myths

Regional settings and migration histories

The 2001 Albanian census revealed the scale of Albania's emigration during the 1990s, and its regional impact.[73] Overall, there was a net migration of 600,000 since the previous census in 1989, even higher if temporary absentees of less than one year are included. As also noted earlier, this very considerable demographic loss – equivalent to one fifth of the population in 2001 – can be seen as a response to the increase in poverty and vulnerability brought about by the collapse of the communist regime and its centralised, protective but repressive apparatus. The migration also perhaps represented a symbolic reaction against the fierce denial of the right to migrate during the 45 years of communist rule.

Although there are geographical contrasts in fertility rates within Albania – higher in the north, lower in the south – the major factor dictating regional variations in population change is migration, both internal and international. Economic crisis and political changes stimulated large-scale flows of emigrants, particularly to Greece and Italy, but internal movements, which were very limited before 1990, have had, if anything, a greater impact on demographic change at the local and district levels. This mixing of internal and international mobility has produced quite a complex regional typology of migratory change in Albania.

In order to appreciate the regional significance of this migratory movement, it is important to measure it against variations in the density of the Albanian population in its various districts. This enables us to understand the complex way in which internal migration and international out-migration have emerged as parallel and combined strategies of survival for Albanian households in the post-1991 period. First, rural-urban migration has accelerated. Although Albania is still the country in Europe with the highest percentage of rural population, internal migration has impacted dramatically on the process of urbanisation of Albanian society, the urban population rising from 36 per cent of the total in 1989 to over 45 per cent in 2001. This has reinforced, at a macro level, the main geographical contrast in Albanian population density, with the majority of the Albanian population historically concentrated in the central and coastal area stretching between the districts of Lezhë in the north and Fier in the south, and comprising at its core the large cities of Tirana, Durrës and Elbasan. In this triangular area, the population density is over 140 inhabitants per square kilometre (Figure 3a). By contrast, the mountainous districts in the northern and southern extremities of the country have historically been sparsely populated, with less than 70 inhabitants per square kilometre. The most thinly populated districts are on the borders with neighbouring countries.

In the absence of net emigration data by district in the published census results, the regional impact of migration can be mapped in two ways. First, simple popula-

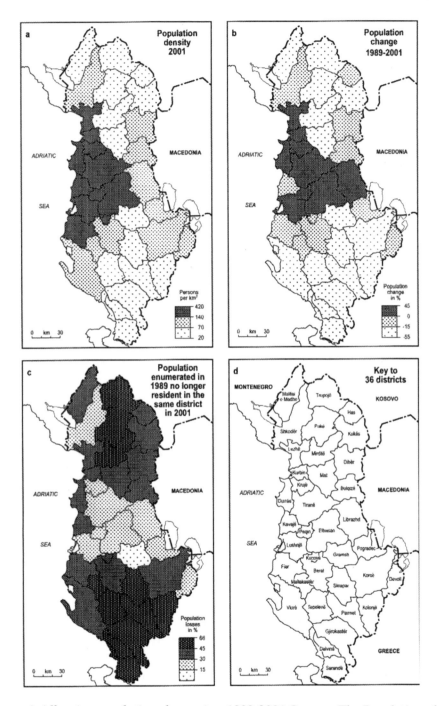

Figure 3 Albania population dynamics, 1989-2001 Source: *The Population of Albania in 2001. Main Results of the Population and Housing Census.* Tirana: INSTAT, 2002

tion change between 1989 and 2001 can be plotted (see Figure 3b). Given that natural change (births minus deaths) remains positive in Albania, total change gives a clear indication of the pattern of out-migration. The national population change during 1989-2001 was a loss of 3.6 per cent. As Figure 3b shows, extreme variations occurred around this national figure, ranging from Tirana (+45.2 per cent) in central Albania to Delvinë (-54.7 per cent) and Sarandë (-45.2 per cent) in the south and Tropojë (-37.6 per cent) in the north. In general the population losses are higher in the south, where they are reinforced by significantly lower fertility than in the northern part of the country.

The second method (Figure 3c) plots the percentage of the population enumerated in 1989 who were no longer recorded in the same district in 2001. This percentage loss is due to death (but this accounts for only 7 per cent of the 'exodus') or out-migration, either to another district or abroad. Figure 3c shows an almost identical spatial pattern to 3b. In both the extreme north and the far south, in several districts, more than 45 per cent (in some cases up to 66 per cent) of the population registered in 1989 were not present in the same district twelve years later. Districts with lower indices – with a greater ability to 'hold on' to their population – form a belt across the centre of the country from Tirana through Elbasan to Pogradec, plus the large northern city of Shkodër.

Comparing the maps in Figure 3, it is clear that migration, both external and internal, acts to sharpen existing contrasts in population density, above all because of migration to Tirana and other main urban centres. The sparsely populated rural upland districts, especially in the far north-east and in the south, get further emptied of their limited populations, whilst the Tirana urban region accumulates more people. This happens both via direct internal relocation, and indirectly, by emigration abroad and return.

From this brief analysis of migration trends and changes in population density over the period 1989-2001, we can identify three main migration regions, corresponding to different socio-economic contexts and producing different migration trajectories:

■ In the southern districts, south of Vlorë, Berat and Korçë, the main reason for the very sharp loss in population was emigration, particularly to nearby Greece. Of the total loss due to district-level out-migration, three-quarters was due to emigration, only a quarter to internal moves. Rural depopulation has been intense and land abandoned wholesale. The cultivation of some abandoned land has been taken up by migrants from northern Albania, where poverty levels are higher.

- In northern Albania, especially the inland, north-eastern districts (Tropojë, Pukë, Kukës, Dibër, Mirditë and Mat), there have been two types of out-migration: a high level of internal migration towards the Tirana-Durrës-Krujë region of central Albania; and external migration direct to Italy, Greece, the UK and other destinations. North-east Albania is the poorest area of the country due to limited employment opportunities and low incomes, which derive mainly from agriculture.

- The central region, especially the Tirana-Durrës axis, is the urban administrative core of the country, containing Albania's largest city and its main port. During 1989-2001 there was an increase of about 45 per cent in the urban population of this central region as a consequence of the influx of migrants from most parts of Albania, but especially from the north. Hence the third regional migration trajectory combines strong inward migration with emigration flows to the main destinations noted above.

From the fieldwork in London we had learned that most Albanians in the UK originated from northern Albania, either moving abroad direct from their home region, or in some combination with an internal move to the outer reaches of the Tirana-Durrës urban area. Few migrants in the UK originated from the south of the country. Our fieldwork in Albania was guided by these migration linkages, and confirmed them. Therefore although we travelled widely around the country, and carried out a handful of interviews in the south, our main fieldwork was concentrated in the north (around Shkodër and Burrel) and in the centre (the peri-urban areas outside Tirana and Durrës). These two regions provide very different settings for emigration, remittances and return.

Migration as a route out of poverty in the mountainous north
Regional data show that northern Albania, especially the north-east, has the highest rates of unemployment, the lowest incomes, the highest incidence of poverty, and the greatest reliance on state social assistance, of all areas of the country. Some of the social indicators were mapped out in greater detail earlier, especially the distribution of poverty on page 36. As the main industrial and productive activities (wood, extraction and hydro-power stations) were either closed down or privatised during the abrupt transition, most families were left with no other resources than their agricultural land. The impact of the closure of state-managed firms on the local economy was typically evident in the case of the village of Koman, whose inhabitants used to be employed in the local hydro-power station. This was recently privatised and only a few of the people who used to work there were able to keep their

jobs. Nowadays, many people in this village and elsewhere live only by the income they make from the products they cultivate on the land area which was assigned to them in the post-communist period. Unfortunately, this is usually limited in quantity and of very low quality.

Northern Albania is also renowned for its cultural and social conservatism, which is reflected in the widespread presence of extended family households and in the resilience of customary law in regulating both the life-cycle of the family and relations between different extended families. A middle-aged man in the village of Mamës spelled out the importance of the family for him and his village:

Family is the regulator of people … life does not finish with us … you have to think about the future, about the continuity of your bloodline. I think you are a human being only if you have family. Time spent without a family for me is lost, wasted. It is for the family that it is worth sacrificing one's labour, one's youth. It is only worth it if it is for the family. … We are a bit worried now about the son who lives in the UK. He keeps telling me: 'wait a bit more, wait a bit more, I am not ready yet'. And we wait, but he is already 25, by this age he should have children already. I did not want him to go there, not at all. Without family? Never. Why would you want to migrate if not to start a new family? What other reason could there be?

NM: But has your son got a girlfriend, I mean, who should he marry if he hasn't got anybody at the moment?

I'll find one for him, from the village, a good girl, no problem. If you want I can find one for you as well, no problem! (general laughter). … It is true that here in the north we are different from the rest of the country, for the fact that many families were involved in feuds, that living conditions were harder and therefore illnesses more serious, one was forced to have many children, as some would die in one way or another. Even in Shkodër it is different from here, they marry later.

In another village the head of an extended family network gave the following revealing account of the impact of the socio-economic conditions on the decision to migrate and vice versa. He also explained how the family feuds which re-emerged with the collapse of communism had become a driving force behind the emigration of many Albanian young men from the area.

I am the head of [this village], which is inhabited by 1,500 people, about 350 families. This is a very isolated place, far up in the mountains. Nobody is unemployed here, but life is very difficult. Each family has only got about 350 square metres of land to cultivate. ... Because of these living conditions ... no water in the place, isolation, very little electricity, the land is also not very fertile ... many people left the village. Usually it is young people of around 20 who leave first ... they go to Greece, but also to Italy and the UK. Overall there are three families in the UK, but more than 70 in Italy and Greece. Half of these young men left for economic reasons, while the other half left to escape revenge. ... With democracy many old wounds reopened and many families decided to leave to escape the consequences. Usually, when families leave to escape revenge, they leave for good as all male members of the family might get killed...about 18 families were forced to leave because of this.

NM: But what happens if they are repatriated?

They will get killed, because such is the law and they are in trouble because they have done something wrong.

While migration is practically the only strategy of survival available to the families of the region, its impact – depopulation of entire villages and municipalities – is destructive, as this father of six children, all living abroad, told us.

How many people live in Burrel now? ... Well, I don't know about the whole of Burrel, but what I do know is that in my neighbourhood there used to be 25 families. Now there are only five and I know for sure that they will be leaving soon. If you go there now you will be frightened, only abandoned land and houses, nobody there, I mean nobody, everybody has gone.

All of the families we interviewed in the north matched the general scenario outlined above. Most of the households were composed of two or three generations, with between six and ten members, the majority women, children and elderly people. Amongst the females were often the wives of emigrant sons, since the wife becomes a member of the husband's household according to the virilocal nature of Albanian customary law. The families lived on the products of their own land, which usually stretched around the family house. Most of the families were living in conditions of visible poverty and were dependent on income benefits, but most of all on remittances, for their survival. The importance of migration as a survival strategy was reflected in the absence of young males from the households we visited. They were all involved in migration to different countries – Greece (the majority), Italy or the UK. In fact, all the families we interviewed had one or more members working in Greece. Migration to Greece is usually temporary and is extremely widespread in this area, despite the long distance from the Greek border. Generally it takes the form of small groups of young males walking for several days the whole length of Albania, and then on across the Albanian-Greek border. Accounts of abuse and violence from the Greek army are quite common, backing up the testimony of Besnïk quoted earlier. In several case histories we collected, migration to Greece was a strategy of acquiring financial capital and experience in order to plan a more ambitious and longer-term migration to another Western country, such as Britain. At the same time, many northern Albanian families were pursuing a parallel, internal migratory strategy to secure their long-term future in Albania.

The interlocking of international and internal migration: the peri-urban spaces of Tirana and Durrës

The region composed of the three urban areas of Tirana, Durrës and Krujë is the main focus of internal migration, especially from the northern and north-eastern parts of the country. Within this growing urban region, with the airport at its heart, one can distinguish two main areas: the Tirana-Durrës axis, along which most industrial and commercial activities are concentrated; and the peri-urban spaces outside Tirana and Durrës, where tens of thousands of migrants have moved since the first post-communist years. The region is extremely heterogeneous as it encompasses the richest and some of the poorest and most socially disadvantaged areas of the country, the latter especially associated with peri-urban squatter settlements. In surveying these peri-urban areas around Tirana and Durrës we wanted to understand both the complex interconnections between internal and international migration, and the way these lead to new forms of social exclusion. We carried out 10 interviews in Katundi i Ri, Porto Romano and Rinia (around Durrës), and 12 interviews in Kamza, Bathore and Breglumasi, the three main peri-urban areas of Tirana.

Although their industrial and productive capacities were heavily affected by closure, dismissal and privatisation, since 1991 the districts of Durrës and Tirana have been attracting both foreign and domestic investment in industry. Here too, the state and, most of all, the construction industry, offer the best and most buoyant employment opportunities in Albania. In the context of the post-communist weakening of state power, the closure and abandonment of large state-managed industrial or agricultural complexes on the fringes of the two urban centres after 1991 gave many families the possibility to relocate from impoverished areas such as northern Albania. In addition, the districts of Tirana and Durrës have large expanses of fertile arable land which was also an important factor in the relocation of many rural families to the area. The hope of finding better educational, health, social and employment opportunities encouraged many families to settle in the

Tirana and Durrës peri-urban areas by illegally occupying former industrial and agricultural compounds. For those who came from the mountainous north and interior, a more benign climate was also an incentive to relocate. This interviewee cleverly summed it all up by reference to an Albanian proverb:

Where are the inhabitants of my village now? Here they are, where else? They are all between Tirana and Durrës. … There is an old proverb in Albania which goes 'close to the King, close to the sea' … it means that if you are close to the government you are more likely to work something out for yourself … whereas the only other possibility is to keep near the sea, to leave the country, to get out … so I guess that is why we all thought to move to Tirana or Durrës in order to live better and have both opportunities. … Here the land is very fertile and the climate is not so bad as up there.

Most families sold their village houses in order to built a new one in this area: sons often migrated in order to send remittances to complete the construction. Usually the migration of a member of the family is seen as an important chance for the whole family and all available resources are pooled in order for the migratory project to be successful, as this account from Kamza, outside Tirana, details:

We used to live in Burrel, in the region of Mat. When democracy arrived, we all lost our jobs there and families started to come down here little by little. First young men went, then the rest of the family followed. This is what we did as well, we sold everything and came down here … the first floor of this house was built by selling the place in Burrel. The second and third floors were built thanks to the money my two grandsons sent from the UK. … It was expensive to send them there … we borrowed some money from our neighbours … then all of the money the two boys had saved from Greece.

The magnitude of this internal migratory pattern is impressive. According to official records the population of Tirana increased from 368,000 in 1989 to 520,000 in 2001;[74] however, according to some unofficial estimates, the Tirana urban area contains 800,000 people.[75] The confusion over the extent of the increase is because many recent in-migrants are not registered, so their precise numbers are unknown. Moreover, the unplanned nature of this migration and settlement has left the new peri-urban areas quite detached from the towns themselves. Because of the lack of infrastructures and services, some rural-urban migrants find themselves living in worse conditions than those they left behind. As many of these areas have neither schools nor social service facilities, illiteracy has begun to grow, while the lack of sewage and health services has been responsible for an upsurge in infectious diseases.[76] In the words of one 65-year-old woman we interviewed at Katund i Ri, outside Durrës,

Well, to tell you the truth, the living conditions were much better in Kukës ... we had our jobs and land, but then everything changed and we were forced to leave ... but now we are in trouble, we even have to borrow money to eat.

In communist times Katund i Ri used to be an important agricultural centre, renowned for its fertile soil and mild climate. In addition, near the locality of Porto Romano, there used to be one of the biggest chemical plants in Albania. As more and more families illegally occupied previously state-owned land, a new scattered conurbation was formed, lacking any infrastructure, services or assistance from the local government. Although these factors have created new processes of social exclusion, leading to the emergence of new vulnerable groups, from the environmental point of view the situation is even worse in the two localities of Porto Romano and Rinia. In Porto Romano many families have settled within the perimeter of the former chemical plant; new houses are mushrooming surrounded by toxic waste. In the locality of Rinia, many families squatted land close to the town pit. Here the difference between those who have and those who do not have relatives abroad is dramatically evident. Families without remittances live in shacks made of metal and wood, and some of them are forced to sell the pieces of metal and other scraps they find in the rubbish tip in order to survive.

In Katund i Ri and Kamza alike, all of the families interviewed were from northern Albania, mainly from the districts of Mat, Kukës and Shkodër, which are amongst the poorest in the country. Therefore most of the demographic, social and cultural traits of those areas have been transported southwards and have continued to play a key role in shaping the phenomenon of migration. This could be seen in two main aspects. Firstly, the size of most of the northern migrant households was noticeably larger than the average of the area. Secondly, the social institutions and cultural practices of the contexts of origin, including extended family networks, were still active within the relocated households.

This second aspect is very important for the purposes of the research, as the extent to which people are embedded within family ideology, networks and institutions shapes both the planning of the migratory project and the remittance behaviour associated with it. We have already mentioned the way the virilocal nature of the Albanian kinship system influences remittance behaviour. It is important to underline how the custom according to which the younger son inherits the family house, but must eventually live with and take care of his parents, shapes the pattern of migration and contributes to family household survival. Here is an interview extract from an elderly couple in Breglumasi, part of the peri-urban zone of Tirana:

How do I feel about the fact that my kids are all gone away? How can I feel, but sad. But then again I look around me and see that 80 per cent of the people who live here are in the same condition, only old people, women and kids live here.

MD: Aren't you afraid to remain alone here? Did you ever ask them to come back?

Well, how can we do that, what possibilities can we offer them?

Wife: All you need is a bit of co-operation in these cases ... we decided all together that the son who is in Greece will return with his family for a couple of years, until the younger one returns from Italy. We will not be alone, he will come and live with us with his wife and kids until the other one returns. ... What can we do? ... We are old ... we cannot go and live abroad at our age.

With these background notes on the two main migration settings in northern and central Albania in mind, we now analyse the receipt and use of remittances from migrants in the UK.

Receiving and managing remittances

Here we examine how remittances are received and managed within the Albanian 'residual' household. Gender and generational contrasts feature prominently in this discussion, as we shall see. This, and the next subsection on the use of remittances, also enable us to cross-check the information presented earlier, where we discussed remittance behaviour from the UK perspective. The research findings do indeed tally, with interviewees in Albania supporting the findings in the UK. This reassuring triangulation also held for other aspects of the migration process, such as family structures, reasons for departure, routes followed, and the key role played by prior migrations to Greece and Italy. In our Albanian field survey, typically it was fathers and mothers who talked about their sons' migratory projects, and amongst many we collected, the following interview extract is typical:

He [26-year-old son] used to live in Greece, in Veria, where there is a lot of work in the fields ... then with the money he made there he went to Italy with a friend. He went there from Vlorë, by speedboat. Once there he worked, he stayed at a cousin's place in the South of Italy and saved the money to go to the UK. He paid somebody 300 US dollars to go to the

UK in a lorry. It was very tiring, he had to stay inside for five days because the French police stopped it. The driver was arrested for some reason, but they did not get caught and eventually got to the UK. There were three friends with him and all they had was a bottle of water. They survived by chance (father, mid 40s, Lushnjë).

As well as individual migration trajectories sequenced in the way described above (first Greece, then Italy, then the UK), it was very common for residual households in Albania to have children scattered simultaneously in several countries:

This house has got five members involved in emigration: one is in England, another in Belgium, two are married in Greece and another one, still unmarried, is also in Greece. It was built by my father many years ago and we decided not to invest any more money here, it is very old and then ... who is going to live here? If my sons come back and for all of our children we have built a new house in Shkodër ... and one in Tirana. ... I think that is where most of the family will go. This house will be left to my younger son, who will take care of us [mother and father] as is our custom, while the rest of my children will have to move away at some stage (father, middle-aged, Mamës, northern Albania).

Clearly the sequencing of migration stages and the distribution of working family members in different countries govern the pattern and amount of remittances flowing back. Although our field survey was limited to households with one or more members in Britain, in nearly all cases at least one other family member was working in Greece or Italy. Our oldest interviewee, Ali, aged 95, originally from the north but now living in Bathore, likened Greece to a bank where one went to get some quick cash:

Greece is like a bank for Albanians, it's where Albanians go to make money whenever they need it. ... I am pretty sure all my sons and grandsons have been there at least once...

But it is also important to underline how, in some households, remittances are not the only income for the family. In these multi-resource households, contributions may also come from other sources such as pensions, social assistance or wages from work available locally. Here is a good example of a multi-income household in Kamza, near Tirana:

We do not live only on the money they send us from abroad, I also have my pension, which is a good one, more than 17,000 Lek per month, because I was an officer for many years. My daughter-in-law works as well, she is a nurse in a nearby hospital ... the two grandsons are in the UK, then my son is a mechanic here in Kamsa. … I mean, if you add all of these things together, that is how you can live.

Quotes such as the one above show the economic strength and social solidarity of the family unit – something that was stressed to us time and again. This interviewee, a middle-aged man from Mamës, made the point forcibly:

Look, you have to understand something. The mentality here is very different from the one in the developed world you live in, because an immigrant, even if he earns money with great sacrifice, has to look back to his family and its most important needs … which are, firstly, the house, the living conditions … then marriages, funerals and stuff like that. Not only the members of a family must take responsibility, but all relatives are responsible and must help each other, uncles, cousins, grandmothers, grandfathers, small children, they all are part of the same picture. Nobody helps you but your family.

Such socially-integrated, supportive family structures may have their advantages in the context of shared hardship and a common household strategy of migration for some family members, but they are generally predicated on a strong patriarchal authority. In virtually all of the household interviews we carried out, the main interviewee was the male head of the family, who was also the person receiving the remittances and administering the whole of the family budget. As within any patriarchal setting, women usually have an important function in the management of the material life of the household, but do not take part in the decision-making. However, with migration of sons comes a subtle inter-generational sharing of decision-making about the management and deployment of remittances, as the following interview extract, recorded in the northern village of Koman, illustrates:

NM: Who gets the money coming from abroad?

Father gets it (chorus).

Yes, I get it and put it into the account. But I spend it for the family, according to what my sons say as well. When they are here, they decide what they do with the money directly. Sometimes I disagree about priorities. For instance I would have rather built a new cowshed instead of buying this new washing machine for my wife, but my son came and started saying 'we must get rid of this old wreck' and that was it. What can I say? After all it's their money we are talking about.

As far as the patriarchal and prescriptive nature of relationships within the household are concerned, these seemed to be internalised by women and men alike. But often, the state of privation these families were living in – especially in northern Albania – made our questions about potential conflicts in decision-making somewhat redundant. In two cases, when women were asked directly if they might have preferred to use the money received from abroad differently, the senior female member of the households practically ridiculed us by saying:

Would I have liked to use it (the money) differently? I do not understand. Do you mean we do not need windows or a door? Or we do not need to eat? We don't need to be warm? There are not that many decisions to take when you live like this.

Who decides? It is the man who decides as usual ... but the real problem is that we do not have enough money, we need much more, although our sons are doing all they can to help us.

Much the same picture emerged with the interviews in the settlements around Tirana and Durrës, since in all cases we were talking to families who had migrated from the north, as well as having family members in the UK. Again, males played the leading role in all cases. But as was pointed out above, the basic survival-bound character of the decisions to be taken makes the issue of management of power within the family look somewhat redundant, especially from the perspective of the interviewees. Usually it is the father who decides how to spend the money 'for the sake of the family'. However, the person who remits can also be a leading actor in the decision-making process as the money sent home is often considered an investment for his own future; how it is used depends also on the real or imagined direction of the migrant life trajectory. The following three excerpts demonstrate variations on this theme. The first, from a 50-year-old man in Rinia, outside Durrës, represents the most uncompromising attitude:

What do you mean who decides? I decide.

NM: And your wife?

She hasn't got a problem ... there is no difference in the way we see life between us.

The second excerpt (interview with a middle-aged couple in nearby Porto Romano) illustrates a slightly more yielding attitude, but also makes the point that when money is short and life is hard, the priorities are clear-cut, and there is not much to discuss:

Who decides the way money is spent? Well, in this family it is me who decides ... over there [i.e. in the UK] they can do what they want. They decide everything about their own places, I mean the ones they built here. We opened two separate accounts so that they find it when they come back. If I need money I just phone them and it can be here in ten minutes, through Western Union.

NM: What about your wife, what about if she needs something different? Does she phone them and ask for money too in the same way?

No, I phone. A couple of times she phoned, but we had agreed on what to ask first.

Wife: We do not disagree on these matters, it is only the two of us and look around, what can we want?

Finally, for this elderly father, interviewed in Bathore, outside Tirana, the younger son had taken over as chief decision-maker:

Who decides? My younger son, he is now in charge of everything ... when they [sons living in the UK] want to do something they phone him up and then they decide, altogether, because this place will be left to them.

NM: What about the mother, does she decide anything?

Of course she is there as well when they talk and she says what she thinks ... and she runs the place, the housekeeping economy of the family.

NM: But does she decide or not?

Well, I give you an example, if they decide that we need some beer, then it is up to her to decide which brand to buy.

All of the families kept in touch with their relatives abroad via mobile phones, which were in all cases the only telephone line for the household, given the under-development of the terrestrial network in Albania. Usually it was the member of the family abroad who phoned the family in Albania, at intervals which varied from around once a week to once a month. In all of the cases we surveyed, money from the UK is sent via Western Union or via banks, whereas family members living in Greece either transfer their money via banks (if they are documented), through friends or neighbours, or carry it themselves when visiting their families during summer or Christmas holidays. Here is a typical response from an interviewee in Mamës to the question about the means of remitting money:

Well, it depends, my two sons living in Greece have documents and so they can travel and bring the money here themselves. The one living in the UK hasn't got papers yet and sends what he can through Western Union. Sometimes, when they cannot come themselves, those in Greece send the money through to the bank in Shkodër, one hour away by car. ... It happens often because the Greeks make problems all the time when renewing the documents and so they cannot come here sometimes for a whole year, like last year. Two of my married daughters have their husbands in Greece and they cannot go and live with them yet as they do not have any kind of document. It's already been three years, living apart.

Usually, the amount sent home is not fixed, but varies according to the contingent possibilities of the migrant and the necessities of the receiving household. As we saw above, this often combines remittances with other sources of income or sustenance, such as production from agriculture or a small state pension. In the words of a father from Koman, in northern Albania:

They do not send the same every month, it depends on their problems and on ours too. In a year we normally get 200,000 Lek and this is enough for us all to live. We get a pension of 7,000 Lek per month and there are nine of us. With this money we can buy basic stuff ... coffee, sugar and flour. With what we receive from abroad we first pay back the money we had to borrow to keep buying food, and then we buy some furniture and some clothes. That's it.

In most cases, we could not determine the actual amount sent as people were either unable or reluctant to quantify it. However, from many interviews it emerged that the amounts sent tend to decrease as the family member living abroad integrates into the host society and subsequently raises his or her expectations about staying there. This is especially true when the migrant marries and starts a new family unit. Another interviewee from northern Albania:

My two older sons, those who still live in Greece, sent the money for the reconstruction of the family house ... they used to send more money in the beginning ... now they have kids of their own, they have families and needs of their own. … Now it is the youngest one, the one who is in England, who helps us more. … They give him accommodation and food there, so he earns quite a lot and he is really helping us all.

Use and impact of remittances

Earning remittances through emigration is seen by most Albanians as the most effective way to escape poverty at the individual and household level.[77] Albanian migrants working abroad have sent home remittances variously estimated to be somewhere between $300 million and $1 billion per annum: the country's major source of external income after aid. Put another way, the remittances sent by one Albanian migrant are equivalent to 2.5 times the sum of the average wages of all members of a family.[78]

How, then, do Albanian migrants and their families back home use the considerable sums of remittances which flow back to the country of origin, and what are the impacts of these capital flows on individual, household and community development?

Most of the dwellings we visited were very modest, but big enough to accommodate a larger number of people than those actually living there. In all cases remittances were used to improve the living conditions of the household. This involved various small projects: moving the toilet indoors; repairing windows, doors and roofs; and buying new furniture and key domestic appliances such as television sets, washing machines and, less often, small electricity generators. In fact the electricity grid is in very poor condition and some families reported having access to electrical energy only for an average of 3-4 hours per day. None of the places we visited used to have access to water in the house before they could afford to install new pipelines with money remitted from abroad. The following example is from the northern village of Koman:

This house was really poor before they left. We spent all of the money rebuilding it really. There were only walls, no windows, nothing. Even the roof had to be repaired. Everything you see here, everything we own, except the bare walls, we could only afford thanks to the sacrifice of my sons.

All over Albania, the story is the same: the first priority for remittances is the basic survival needs of the family and an improvement in the quality of accommodation and facilities. Down at the coast, on the open plain at Katund i Ri, north of Durrës, it was easy to distinguish those houses inhabited by families who did not receive remittances from those with family members living abroad.

In this area there are about 15 people abroad, the majority in the UK, but only the younger ones have managed to get documents ... the others are all being repatriated. ... Why have they left? To help their families! I only get 6,000 Lek per month. ... There are 11 of us in this house – how could we survive? That is the only possibility, otherwise we would have to borrow money even to eat, and that has happened in the past. All of us, all our families can only survive because we get money from abroad. The living conditions cannot be compared: those with relatives abroad live in houses, the others live in shacks.

The living conditions for those who do not receive any remittances are very hard, as this woman living in a shack nearby told us:

Well, what can I say? ... We live in a shack ... we live in very difficult conditions ... eight people together ... we have nobody abroad. My only son is married and lives here with his wife and three daughters. We live on social support, about $25 per month for all of us. We try and make do with what we have. I bake bread in the oven at home, we live with what the orchard produces. We don't have water, or electricity. My son can't leave because he is the only man in the family here ... now he is unemployed and we have problems ... we are lucky if he gets work one day a week.

Alongside the improvement of the basic living conditions of the household, other priorities are related to the necessity to secure the respectability of the extended family, by allowing them to celebrate baptisms, weddings and funerals appropriately. These events are hugely important as they mark the history and progression of the family household and are usually the occasion at which different families negotiate and demonstrate their respectability and honour in relation to their immediate socio-economic context. These issues are brought out well in this interview in Mamës:

When the older son came to visit us from Greece the first time, he fixed the water pipeline to the house ... the younger one also came back from Greece and offered to move the toilet indoors and to improve the kitchen with new appliances ... then we had to marry four daughters and that is a lot of money ... about £2,000 each .. that's British pounds, because it was our son in England who helped us with the last marriage. I mean, all of this furniture, everything you see here, the television set, the heater, this sofa you are sitting on, we bought it all thanks to their work abroad.

However, the sending and spending of remittances also depend on often complex combinations of factors to do with earning capacities, legal status in the destination country, and the shifting plans of the migrants to stay abroad, form new families (abroad or at home), or return. As ever, gender roles cross-cut many of these processes. This next testimony from the mother of two sons living in Italy and the UK, reveals how both the way that remittances are spent, and the migratory project as a whole, are shaped by hegemonic family patterns, gender roles and economic necessities.

I have two sons and three daughters. Only the two younger daughters are here with me now, they are still at school. One son is in the UK, the other is in Italy, with his sister. He is the one who could help us more, as he can rely on his sister for everything. She cannot help us as she has got her life. ... I mean she is married and must help her new family. She sends us some presents, but that is all she can do personally ... but she also helps us in other ways because she takes care of her brother and organises everything. Because he lives with her, he gives her everything he earns, and then she saves some for us and gives him back something for his everyday life ... she is like a 'regulator'. The one in the UK now has lost the assistance and has got to pay for everything. So now he is not helping much, but he used to send so much money before. ... I mean there was nothing here before my children left, and with the money they all sent we brought the water to the house, bought new furniture and a new heater, we improved the little food shop I run ... and we even bought a piece of land in Shkodër to build a new house for when we will be old and the children will be back, if they will ever be back.

At the end of the above extract there is reference to future plans to move to Shkodër, the main town in northern Albania. Other interviewees also referred to similar projects, demonstrating how international migration can be used to finance an internal migration to a place seen as more desirable for the family's future. Here is another example of migration planning which sees the sequence reversed: first, an internal move away from the remoteness of village life in northern Albania to a place in central Albania which then acts as a platform both for a better life for the family as a whole, and for the emigration of some of its younger members. The example is from Katund i Ri:

We moved from Tropojë to Durrës in 1992. Then my older son went to Greece for six months. He did not like it there but he helped us a lot ... thanks to him we built a new home from scratch ... before we used to live in a shack made of wood and metal ... He then went to Italy and sent money from there too. Now he lives in London, he's been there two years.

But as sons and daughters emigrate, they may get married and form their own families abroad, at which point their remittances are either lost or decrease markedly. The inevitability of this was accepted by the interviewees in Albania – after all, for their children to get married is exactly what they would want – but it also raised questions about whether they will return, and if so, to where in Albania. A return to the harsh mountains of northern Albania is seen as obviously problematic, since the developmental potential of this region remains limited; resettlement in the more urbanised lowland of central Albania may be more attractive, as with this family:

My son is very interested in the construction of the house ... he wants it to be complete and wants to know everything about it ... because he wants to come back here to live, and marry. He told me recently that he just wants to make some money there [in the UK] and then open his own construction firm here ... to be a builder here (father, Rinia, near Durrës).

Even in this more developed part of Albania, parents are sceptical about whether their sons and daughters will return. The next interview extract, from Breglumasi (Tirana), shows a typical case of how, after a first phase in which the migrant sends home as much as he can to improve the living conditions of the entire family unit, he then starts investing in his own family, building a separate household close to the parents' house. It also shows how the purpose of houses built from remittances changes along with the migratory project. When the reality of returning becomes more unlikely, these houses become signifiers of belonging and proof of achievement, to be enjoyed only during visits or holidays.

In the beginning the first son helped us a lot, me and my wife, but then he started thinking about his own family and sent 100,000 Lek to get his wife and his children to the UK. ... Then he helped his brother and his little sister, she's still going to school, with money. With the money he sent us we fixed the place ... overall we spent about 300,000 Lek to improve it, new furniture and stuff, but then we also had to go to hospital and that was where the rest of the money went. However, each of the three brothers built a place for when they will be back ... for holidays I mean ... because if they get documents they will all stay abroad ... they will not come back for real ... they will live and work there and return here more often.

Alongside the obvious use of foreign earnings for day-to-day living expenses and improvement of housing and other material aspects of life, we also investigated whether migrant households were using remittances to finance a business project or to invest in the education of children. We found very little convincing evidence of meaningful business investment of remittance income in northern Albania. These two examples of modest agricultural improvement and expanding a shop reveal the limited horizons of business development in this part of the country:

Well, we hired somebody with better tools, in order to work the land deeper. We do not have the tools or the strength to work the land. … I am the only man in the family and I am over 70 years old. … Then we bought some better seeds. … But we lack an irrigation system here and it is very hard work to carry the buckets from the well around the field. We bought a pig once, to feed him up and then eat him, but he used to eat more than all of us together!

Did we invest the money they sent from the UK to improve our economic conditions? Well, not much, but we did something. We improved the shop and then we brought water to the orchard and we replanted the vines … in the end we did get more from the land, but only for us. I had opened the shop before they [the sons] left, but their money was important to make it bigger and better.

Down on the coast and around the main towns of Albania the prospects for a more productive investment of migrant remittances are only marginally better. In fact, in these areas we recorded a variety of experiences. On the one hand, the small scale of the remittances available (particularly after living and housing costs have been taken care of) and the lack of infrastructure pose what are seen as insuperable obstacles to investment, as these two brief extracts testify:

If I had the money I would open a shop or a bar. I don't want to work for other people any more. … But the reality is that the money from the UK only comes every now and then. … Since he got married and started his own family he cannot help us much (40-year-old brother of emigrant, Rinia).

What kind of activity could we open here? There are no roads, no water supply; it is not up to us to build these things (man, early 40s, Bathore).

But we also found more positive things happening. The box on page 83 tells the story of George, an Albanian resident in England whom we encountered on one of his return visits to plan the building of a tourist hotel. In Lushnjë, where the land is flat and fertile, we interviewed a middle-aged man who, having worked as an agronomist under communism, was able to start a small agricultural enterprise thanks to the remittances sent by his son living abroad. His family comprised himself and his wife, two sons and one younger daughter. The older son, aged 28, has been living in the UK since 1998 and recently got his documents. He had first emigrated to Italy and from there moved to the UK. After having worked in the informal sector as a waiter for an Italian restaurant in England for three years, he now runs his own restaurant together with his English wife, who used to be his employer. The younger son is 24 and works on the family farm, as does the 14-year-old daughter, who attends the local high school.

The father estimated that the elder son had been able to send home more than $15,000. This capital was first used to improve the living conditions of the family, and then to set up the family-run agricultural enterprise. The money was spent to improve the toilet and the kitchen first, then to purchase some furniture, and finally to begin the construction of the second floor, where the younger son will eventually settle down once married. As regards the family business, the father was able to use his son's remittances to set up greenhouses and equipment to cultivate most of the 1,000 square metres of land owned by the family. He later complemented this source of income by opening a small fertiliser and pesticide shop for local farmers. Now the family lives from the income generated by agricultural production.

Now we are fine, I mean we are normal. My son is not sending anything any more because he has to take care of his own business now, he has his own problems to take care of. ... In the beginning he used to send 200-300 US dollars every month, through Western Union, then little by little he began having his problems and responsibilities over there.

The father takes charge of the economic situation of the family, although decisions and responsibilities are agreed and divided between the family members:

Well, I receive the money and in the end I am the one to make decisions ... but we all take part in decisions, especially my wife, but now also my son, since he is an adult. We have to decide together because we also work altogether. We all work for the same enterprise, our enterprise. My daughter goes to school, but when she comes back she prepares food and cleans the place. My wife takes care of the administration, my son helps me out with every-thing else. Now we are better than when we used to live only on remittances. We earn more and do not need the money from abroad any more.

We now briefly examine the impact of remittances on the education of children of the family. But first, two preliminary remarks about the gender dimension. First, in our interviews with 'residual families', we found it was invariably women who answered questions pertaining to education, reflecting a gendered subdivision of responsibilities within the household. Second, we could not find any evidence of

George's story

This interview illustrates one of the unwritten principles of fieldwork, namely that the best information and the most informative and 'genuine' interviews arise out of chance meetings, without the constraints, 'rules' and artificiality of a purposely set-up interview. This encounter took place late on a Saturday afternoon on the battlements of Berat Castle. George, in the true style of an Albanian young man out to impress, had driven his Mercedes up to the top of the castle ramparts with a young female companion. Overhearing us speaking in English, he opened up a conversation which started with some remarks about the panorama, which was indeed spectacular. When we asked George how he came to speak such excellent English, and he told us he had been living for several years in England, the interview had begun!

George was 30, self-confident, talkative, but also extremely insightful, both as regards what migration had meant for himself, and the transformations and possibilities that were open to Albania. He started off by telling us about the hotel he was planning to build down on the coast: he had already bought the land and the work would begin the following week. He was back in Albania for a few months in order to initiate the project, which he was co-financing with his brother, also a migrant in England. George had started his migratory career in 1991, working in Greece (Zakynthos) for seven summer seasons in the tourist trade, mainly in catering. He had eventually ended up by renting a snack bar with a Greek partner, but in the end it didn't work out, and he pulled out of the venture. Whilst he had found the Greeks friendly in general, he had become frustrated by the limited horizons to which he had been allowed to take his energies and ambitions - he felt he had been held back because of the general Greek negative view of Albanians, and because the tight Greek family and kin structure always prevails, denying Albanians the chances they deserve. However, whilst working in Zakynthos he had also met Tracey, an English girl on holiday with whom he fell in love and whom he was eventually to marry. George then drew out a series of insightful comparisons: between Greece and England, between how Tracey behaved in Zakynthos on holiday and back in England, and between how he saw his own behaviour and identity in different places (Albania, Greece and England).

The two-hour flight between Greece and London he likened to a rapid journey between night and day. Whilst it appeared that his overall experience of working seven summers in Zakynthos had been positive, and he hinted that he had had a good time in various ways, the fact that he was an Albanian migrant worker was always against him. In England, after an initial transition period of settling in (he had his brother already there to help him, plus his relationship with Tracey of course), he discovered that he had really 'found himself'. On several occasions he stressed how in England there was no limit to what he could achieve, irrespective of his ethnicity. This was a country, he said, where people's true value is recognised, in terms of who they are as a person, how hard they work, and how much initiative they show. He had never felt that 'being Albanian' had ever been held against him in England; rather, people's reaction had been along the lines of 'you're from Albania, how interesting ... where's that, exactly, what language do you speak?' He had found the English diffident and somewhat difficult to get to know initially, but through Tracey, his workmates and neighbours, he had got to know many people, and to appreciate their honesty and lack of prejudice. His work had been within the catering sector in various places in and around London. Latterly he had been working as an assistant manager in a restaurant in the City of London, with a salary of £25,000, and had been living in a nice area of North London. He also reminisced about the quaint Suffolk town he had worked in earlier and of the friendliness of local people in pubs he had been in.

George stressed how fond he was of the British way of life, and of how much he had learnt there about different modes of behaviour. He gave particular praise to his 'GM' (general manager), who was always calm, whatever the crisis and whatever the pressures on his time. This had taught George to be more patient and measured in his own reactions and to avoid quick, flare-up reactions which would have been his normal behaviour before. He drew a contrastive comparison between, on the one side, the Albanians and the Greeks, who he said were very similar in this behaviour and in so many other respects, and on the other the British, who were so much more calm, especially where relations with regard to women are concerned, allowing them independence and the right to speak for themselves.

The relationship with Tracey had been an important narrative linking Zakynthos, England and his own learning and identificatory process, leading him away from what he saw as a typical young Albanian male to a more calm, mature, rounded individual. Although he drew a contrast between Tracey's behaviour when in Zakynthos - always drinking too much vodka - and her life back in England linked to the more humdrum relations of work and family, he paid fulsome praise to her role in teaching him to accommodate to and appreciate the 'British way'. Eventually he had married her, but felt that he had been rushed into this before he was psychologically ready, and they divorced after one year, since when they have, however, remained in contact and are on friendly terms. He had been separated from Tracey now for over two years.

In the final part of the conversation, George talked about his feelings for Albania, his family there, and his plans for the future. He told how he had begun to feel the emptiness of his possessions without someone to share them with. He mentioned that he had frequently changed his car in England and how he had recently lavished £1,200 on a sophisticated home entertainment system. Soon after he had bought it, he had sat down to watch it, turned to his right to see an empty chair, and to his left to also see no-one there, and so had begun to question the futility of these possessions if he had no-one to share the pleasure with. Since he had been back in Albania he had bought the car of the 'successful Albanian', a large Mercedes: he had been over to see an uncle in it, and then over to see an aunt, but then again had begun to question the meaning of such possessions. (The girl he was with, who appeared to have a purely ornamental function, remained silent and uninterested throughout the hour-long conversation, or wandered around with a recognisably bored expression. When we expressed concern that our conversation with him was keeping him from enjoying the afternoon with his friend, he dismissed the idea peremptorily, with an off-hand remark about 'Oh don't worry, she's OK…' - our impression, about which we were feeling increasingly guilty, was that she was not very happy about being ignored for so long. Evidently there were some aspects of his unreconstructed Albanian male persona which remained unchanged!).

So, clearly, despite his fondness for, and his ability to 'be himself' and 'find himself' in London, he was inevitably drawn back to Albania, partly over his sympathy for his father who is growing old whilst all four of his children are working abroad. Whilst George (and presumably his brothers and sister) were able to return from time to time and to send money to keep the father going, he felt his future now lay in Albania after the failure of his marriage. Although Albania had been through difficult times and young people were continuing to have to work abroad in order to have anything approaching a decent standard of living, George felt that Albania's medium-term future was assured. 'Make no mistake', he said, 'this country is going to develop'.

Tourism was clearly the sector he had identified as having the biggest contribution to make, and where he was poised to make his own contribution. The hotel would be close to the beach (but not on the beach, since this was now banned and all illegal buildings which had already been built on the sand and in the coastal pinewoods would have to be taken down - George's repeated expression for this was that they had all 'fucked up' and they would have to be destroyed). It would have 52 bedrooms, a restaurant, bar, pool etc. When asked about whether his experience in England as a migrant generally had been useful or instrumental in his new business plan, his answer was unequivocal: of course - this is exactly the result of all my work and experience abroad, not only money to invest in the project, but also languages, how to manage people, how to treat guests and so on.

George's story remains a superb example of a successful Albanian migratory trajectory, although obviously the ultimate economic success of his hotel venture remains to be proven. In the short term he will continue to work in England to finance the project; one imagines that in the long term George will resettle in Albania, see himself as one of the country's most successful hotel entrepreneurs, and hope that he can play his role in - and draw substantial benefits from - Albanian's future development.

gender discrimination in relation to access to schooling: people were adamant that boys and girls in the family should have equal opportunity, and in fact reacted quite vigorously to any suggestions that boys might be favoured.

Education was certainly a priority in family budgeting and in the destination of remittances, but in many cases a more serious problem was that of physical distance from schools. Here is the situation in one of the remote villages we surveyed in northern Albania:

NM: How about education, did you use the money coming from abroad to improve the education of your children?

Mother: Well, the problem is not the money, we could afford it right now, but the service. The school is very far, over one hour by bus, and the bus only comes here once or twice a week, when it comes at all. Then the teachers they send up here are not very good normally and in the end none of these children can go to school regularly.

As a result, access to education often features as part of the decision-making leading to a departure from remote rural areas. Another mother:

Well, right now we cannot move because we have to take care of Father and of this place, but in the future we will move to Shkodër as the daughters have to go to high school. ... Right now they have to walk four hours each day to go to school. I would also like them to attend private courses in foreign languages or computing, but it is impossible here because of the distance. We have invested a lot of money and effort in education; all of my children have at least the high school diploma ... without my sons in the UK we could certainly not afford it, but since they are helping us, they all go to school every morning.

But moving to the peri-urban settlements which sprawl around the main lowland towns does not necessarily improve the situation, as this mother, originally from Kukës, but now living in Rinia, outside Durrës, told us:

Well, all of my children have got the minimum compulsory education – this was while we were living in Kukës. ... Now we cannot afford to send them to high school ... and what education will they get here, amidst mud and poverty? ... Since we moved here we cannot afford to send them ... transportation is expensive. Who has the money to send them to school!? It is 200 Lek per child, in our case it would be over our budget, almost 1,000 Lek per month, we simply haven't got it.

NM: Would you consider sending only boys to school in this situation?

No way, they all have to study, there is no such difference here.

Returning migrants, reintegration and business development

As yet, there is very little definitive return migration to Albania. A process of return had begun to take place, in the mid-1990s, of people who had been part of the first wave of departures to Greece and Italy at the beginning of the decade, but the pyramid crisis of 1997 and the ensuing political chaos interrupted this trend, and drove many returnees abroad once more. Now, six years on, with a measure of economic and political stability emerging, there are the first signs of another phase of return, but it is as yet embryonic. Evidence from UK-based Albanians suggests that much would have to change in Albania before return could be contemplated as an option for many. Furthermore, one has to distinguish between definitive return, when migrants return and resettle long-term, and temporary returns, notably from Greece, which are short-term interludes between periods spent abroad – either shuttling back and forth to Albania's Balkan neighbour, or moving on to new destinations, such as Italy or the UK. A further distinction can be made between voluntary and forced return.

Given the relative recency of Albanian migration to the UK, most migrants having left in the late 1990s, return was something that was talked about but, in the majority of cases, not yet acted upon. Uncertain legal status made repatriation a fear and a possibility for many; yet largely for economic reasons most wanted to prolong their stay, if not indefinitely, at least for some time. For migrants and their families, the much better economic opportunities and social conditions in the UK, compared to Albania, were the key factors militating against return, as will repeatedly emerge in the interview extracts presented below.

We also draw attention to the detailed case study of George, who is planning a return as the owner of a new hotel catering to Albania's future tourist potential. His marriage to (but subsequent separation from) an English woman had given him legal security and his many years of experience in the catering trade had taught him useful skills.

From the perspective of the 'residual family' and especially of the parents of the migrants, there is often the expectation that their sons will return, generally upon marriage, and with the anticipation that they will rejoin the extended family and perhaps start a small business. Family houses are extended and new dwellings built, with migrant remittances, precisely with this plan in mind. This brief interview exchange, in a household near Tirana, provides a typical illustration of these expectations. It reinforces a point made earlier about the relation of remittances to house-building and the eventual destination of the migrant's trajectory; and it shows also how such investment is related to the main rite of passage to adulthood – marriage.

NM: Why is this place so large?

Do you think it is too large?

NM: Well, I would have thought a whole floor would be enough for three people…

Yes, but the other two floors are for my sons, those who live in the UK. … When they get married they will come here to live and open a business. They want to open their own restaurant, or a shop, to be self-employed.

Other interviews reveal a more ambivalent perception – a kind of 'myth of their children's return'. They hope that the children will return, and lay plans accordingly; but they also acknowledge that, both from an economic point of view, and because emigration brings cultural change, return may never happen. In this next extract the father acknowledges the possibility of non-return of his sons, but on the other hand refuses to admit the possibility of cultural change through their emigration to the UK:

They like their life over there … and they don't want to come back. …I have found a wife for one of them but he does not come back … in fact he can't come because he's got no documents. … I haven't seen my sons in four years; if only I had 400,000 Lek I would go there and see them for a week or so.

NM: Aren't you afraid that they will have changed, that maybe now they don't want to marry any more? Maybe they want to live a different life?

No, we don't have these problems here.

However, in a few cases, and usually when it is the mother speaking, another more complex picture emerges.

Well, the first one is very determined [to come back and live in Albania] but the second and the youngest one … they have abandoned our traditions a bit … they say they don't want to marry, especially not an Albanian girl. ... I am not sure they will come back; they say that they like it there.

Parents often complain that the current policy regulating entry into the UK, and into other countries as well, does not allow them to see their children for years. Most parents of migrants have never seen their grandchildren born in the UK, while they could see those born in Greece or Italy. The pain of this separation is brought out in the following interview extract:

Our son, the one who lives in the UK, is the one who overall could help us more but, although the British state was very generous and helped him for two years, they gave him no papers and as a result I have not seen my own son for five years. I have never met my grandchildren ... only if you have children working abroad can you understand what this means. ... I worry all the time and I feel sorry for him and his children because I know what they have to go through (father, Burrel, northern Albania).

The pain of a different kind of separation – of a husband from his wife – was the reason for a hastened return in this case:

I had to come back because of my family, my wife and my children could not carry on anymore without me. It was very difficult you know, they were crying every time I phoned. ... My wife in particular wanted me to return ... she said it was too much for herself alone. I would have stayed two more years to secure a better future for my family. ... I was able to send more money in the beginning, while they gave me a place to stay and money for my basic needs ... they gave me full support for one and a half years ... it was a lot of money ... but it would have been better if they gave me a permit to work instead, so that I could get better wages. Because I had no documents I used to work off the books in the UK and the money was not that great. ... I could not send home much, just to fix the place up a bit. ... If I had had a permit to stay I could have come home and seen my family every three months or so (returnee, Breglumasi, Tirana).

Many families expressed great concern about the increasing number of Albanians repatriated from the UK and the problems this entailed.

I know the UK cannot accept everybody ... but right now they are returning entire families, even worse they are returning women without their husbands ... I mean women with three or four children. ... These children were born in the UK and cannot speak Albanian at all … and the husband is still there, so after a week they try and go back there, what else can they do? (man, 40s, Kamsa).

They repatriated two guys from our family recently. … They stayed here for a month and then left for Italy by ferry. They said it immediately … I cannot live here any more, I am not staying here, I have to go back (man, 50s, Rinia).

This latter excerpt points to another area of concern for 'residual' families: the way their relatives living and working abroad, by adapting to the better living conditions of the country of emigration, are unable to return and live in Albania. The following testimonies give further examples.

When my two sons came back (from the UK) … they could not believe what they saw here. … Now they are used to the conditions over there in the UK … after two days they could not stand it any more and started thinking about going back … they did not say anything of course, but it was plain to see.

So, on the one hand emigration is seen as an opportunity to expand the cultural horizon of the family, but more often this undermines the actual likelihood of return and re-settlement in Albania.

Migration is not only about money, my children learnt about different and more developed places, they opened their eyes to the world (father, Bathore).

When he came back he had changed … he would not throw things on the floor like we do, he would go all the way over to the bin and put them in there, wherever he was. … And when I asked him if he wanted to return, he said 'I don't want my kids to live here' (father, Rinia).

The limited amount that migrants are able to save does not generally enable them to invest in new productive enterprises. The lack of credit facilities and the poor infrastructures are also very important factors preventing Albanian returnees or 'residual' households from setting up larger-scale productive facilities. For this returnee, lack of security, political instability and lack of long-term credit are perceived as the most important factors limiting Albanians' confidence in investing on their own country.

Of course I would like to open a new activity. … But it is not only a question of money … it's also got to do with security. If I had the economic resources I would start my own whole-

sale shop. I actually tried to open a dairy once, because my father used to be a dairyman. With the money I had earned in Greece I bought all the tanks and stuff, but as I was returning home … then the troubles began. … I got afraid and decided to sell everything … it was all ready but then it seemed as if civil war would start again … there were road block-ages and people were robbed along the way. … However, when I did come back I built a cowshed to start producing meat and milk, but we had to close it down as, in order to make money, it needed more investment. … So I decided to open a petrol station, which is not working very well because the road here is in a terrible state and there is not much passing traffic. … If only the government could guarantee some security and some credit to build new economic activities. … I mean long-term credit, not two months, but 10-20 years. I got 4,000,000 Lek from the German bank, but only for two months (35-year-old returnee, Rinia).

Similar arguments were advanced in other interviews. Let us return to the enter-prising farmer in Lushnjë, introduced above. He was asked about the possibilities for returnees to develop new enterprises and whether there was any help or credit available from banks or the state.

Well, nothing really. Because the state is so poor and disorganised that we must help it, not vice versa! (laughs). The thing is, either you have a son abroad who can help you, or nothing, you just stay where you are. Private banks can give money only to people who own something … and you see we own but we don't own, do you get it? There is nobody here who can tell you what you own and so private banks cannot help you at all. I mean they can only offer you short-term loans with very high interest rates, more than 20 per cent. … Who can afford that? All of the people who started businesses here have done so through the help of their relatives abroad. But only a few decide to invest, because this country is still very unstable … do you remember 1997 and all those troubles just a few years ago? Well, people lost their trust and just use money to survive, to eat, they would rather keep it under the bed because they do no trust our state, our politicians. … The memory of the pyramid schemes is still vivid … it is not that people do not have money, they do. But they keep it in a vase because they are afraid to lose it. Not to mention the taxes … they are so high … just because nobody pays them and then those who pay have to do so for everybody else.

The farmer also points to the unresolved issue of land privatisation and the lack of a unified land registry system which prevents people from using their properties as collateral to obtain credit. The interview continued thus:

NM: What kind of activities were started by those who decided to invest remittances by opening a business?

Look, most of them are bars ... food shops ... maybe a bakery ... small, very small.

NM: It is very striking that there is an absence of Albanian products in shops. Earlier today I saw Italian milk for sale in normal shops. Why isn't there Albanian pasteurised milk?

With all the taxes and expenses, and for the fact that the money your relatives can send you is not a lot, all this does not enable the creation of manufacturing industries, which would employ more people... Then you see the prices? They are so high because we have to import everything...even milk!

Economic growth is also undermined by the absence of productive diversification and specialisation as well as of services supporting production and commerce. The farmer, again:

It is not only a problem of production, here the problem for example is that there is nothing around your product. There is no way we can compete on foreign markets as we are now. I mean I usually take my products by bicycle and sell them in bags at the local market. If I were to sell abroad I would have to package it and you know what? There is not a single firm in this country who can do that. I asked around and the cheapest possibility would be to get the packaging from Germany, which would mean that in the end our food would cost more than what we import from abroad already. I mean, couldn't the state fill these gaps in the production system?

It is clear that it is the same factors that propelled Albanians abroad in the first place – poverty, low incomes, economic chaos, lack of infrastructure and reliable utilities – that are also responsible for inhibiting a business-oriented return. The development of new enterprises does occur but it is on a very small scale. Its future progress is hampered by a poor consumer base defined by low incomes and spending capacity, by lack of credit for expansion, and by a lack of basic services such as roads, public transport, electricity, and water, and of business services such as secure credit.

4| Migration and poverty: A viable policy framework

I n this final chapter, we draw out the conclusions from the research and apply these to the migration policy issues facing governments and others in the UK, the EU and Albania. Migration is one of the most high profile – and sensitive – policy issues in public debate in the UK, as well as many other EU countries. Often presented by politicians and media alike simply as a 'problem', the complexities of the issue are elided. Moreover, migration has been presented by some as a policy choice, something which can be 'switched off' with sufficient political will. All the evidence is that this is not the case, that migration is a given and will remain an inevitable feature of a globalising economy for the foreseeable future. The challenge for mature policy making is to ensure that the benefits of migration are promoted and its negative impacts are minimised, both for host countries and the sending countries, and for migrants themselves.

In drawing our policy conclusions, we accept that the experience of Albanian migrants may not be wholly representative of the migratory patterns into the EU or the UK specifically. Albania is just one country, and indeed is a 'special case', both as Europe's poorest country and as the country currently most affected by out-migration. Nor do we suggest that this research constitutes a representative study of the experience of Albania migrants themselves. But, as a case study, the research does provide valuable insights for policy development.

Our analysis of this and other evidence leads us to believe that migration can, if properly managed and facilitated, do three things. It can have positive effects on the labour markets, economies and societies of the host countries in the West. It can provide important sources of finance and human capital in order to stimulate development in the origin countries, such as Albania. And finally, it can be an immensely positive experience for the migrants themselves, above all because of its potential to improve their incomes and livelihoods, and those of their families.

We do acknowledge the deep linkages between migration flows and entrenched patterns of global inequality, which in many cases are historically 'fixed' and reflect the global evolution of capitalism – this issue should be the subject of continuing concern and debate. A 'win-win-win' situation – migration for the benefit of all – may appear utopian, but we believe it is not just a theoretical ideal, and that policies can be framed in such a way that the benefits to all can be enhanced.[79] But we also believe that policy must carefully guard against several negative outcomes of the migratory process especially where, as in the Albanian case, this process is beset by regimes of migration control that appear unnecessarily harsh, by prevailing myths and stereotypes about the nature of international migration and particular migrant groups, and by the reality in which many migrants are left vulnerable and exploited in the host country. The Albanian case also throws up difficult problems in the home country which are obstacles to a positive role for migration in development: above all the disorganised and socially disruptive way in which migration has occurred, and continuing weaknesses in the political and economic structure of the country.

Migration, poverty and development: revisiting the debate in the light of the Albanian evidence

Albania suggests itself as a particularly good case study to illustrate and analyse the interrelationships between migration and return on the one hand, and poverty alleviation and development on the other. Albania is the poorest country in Europe and the one most intensely affected by emigration over the past twelve years. Whilst the academic literature stresses the complexity of these linkages between migration, poverty and development, and argues against simplistic causal linkages, there seems little doubt, on the evidence we have collected, that poverty and political and economic chaos are the main 'drivers' of emigration from Albania. Albanian people feel that emigration is the key to their survival.

However, this is not long-term grinding poverty produced over generations by increasing population pressure or environmental degradation. The poverty of the Albanian people reflects the recent and sudden political and economic chaos which accompanied the country's dramatic exit from a fiercely isolationist communist regime. We would therefore question whether Albania fits the conventional model of European labour migration whereby migrants seek better jobs and improved incomes. Time and again, interviewees told us how, for them, emigration was their only chance for survival. Kosta Barjaba[80] opts for the term 'economic refugees', blurring the conventional binary in current migration debates into 'economic migrant' and 'political refugee'.

So we can be quite clear about the double relationship between poverty and migration in Albania. Poverty – broadly defined – has been (and continues to be) a hugely important factor in Albanian migration. And migration has been equally significant in its impact on alleviating poverty in Albania. Quite apart from the evidence we have gathered in our field interviews in various parts of Albania, other research and survey evidence confirms this link.[81]

What is less clear is the relationship between poverty alleviation (through migration and remittances) and further migration. Is there a 'demonstration effect' whereby migration stimulates further migration as the evidence of improved quality of life (better food, clothing, housing, appliances etc.) becomes visible to other households? Or do migration and return create the economic conditions whereby emigration becomes less necessary? Based on detailed observations in southern Albania, Beryl Nicholson argues that remittances are a means of development, leading people not to migrate, especially when returnees are able to microfinance new initiatives such as improved farming techniques, shops and other services.[82]

Our field evidence, collected in the main in northern and central Albania, and our interviews with migration experts and other key informants in Albania, leads us to be sceptical about migration and remittances functioning as an equilibrating mechanism staunching further migration, at least in the short term and in the specific conditions of northern Albania. Our scepticism is based on the following observations:

- The economic, social and cultural environment for 'development' is still unpropitious in Albania, especially in rural areas and in the north of the country
- Agriculture remains a devastated and disorganised sector in which, apart from isolated local initiatives, it is difficult to foresee returnees and their capital finding good investment opportunities. The rural sector is handicapped by poor or non-existent infrastructures (lack of irrigation, power, roads etc.), tiny farm holdings and the lack of a land register. Moreover, there are very few agricultural processing, packaging and marketing systems, and competition from imported food is a further disincentive to Albanian agricultural development.[83]
- There is an overall deficit in adequate infrastructures – water, electricity, communications, public transport, credit and security – making any kind of private enterprise difficult to initiate for returnees

- As far as Albania-UK migration is concerned, the recency of this migration (mostly within the last 4-5 years) means that there are few returnees as yet. Returns from Italy and Greece, where Albanians have been migrating since 1991, are more common, but still not widespread, due to the poor economic conditions in Albania. Especially from Greece, returnees intersperse periods back home with absences abroad

- Whatever their original intentions, most Albanians who are in the UK now aspire to stay there, at least for the foreseeable future. Hence Albania-UK migration is transforming itself into a one-way process because of the lack of economic opportunities in Albania and migrants' changed attitudes after living in a different environment. Most migrants value the UK's rich and stable economy and declare themselves willing to return to Albania only if 'everything changed' there – an unlikely prospect in the short term

Another key finding of our research is the complex way in which Albanian migration to the UK is embedded within other migration processes, both internal and external. A common pattern was for most migrants to the UK to have already spent some time as a migrant in Greece and/or Italy, using the latter as a springboard for overland travel to the Channel ports, usually via Brussels, where Albanian gangs coordinate the smuggling of migrants in the back of lorries. When discussing migration, many Albanians refer to Greece as the 'key' and Italy as the 'door'. Regarding the interlocking of international migration and internal moves, we found case histories of a number of variations on this theme: international moves followed by internal migration, vice versa, and simultaneous and overlapping migrations by different family members. It is also common for members of the same family to be distributed as emigrants in several countries, such as Italy, Greece, the UK and Germany. These complex typologies of movement and relocation are creative and rational responses to the geography of opportunity structures on the part of Albanian households and families – a kind of do-it-yourself development in the face of limited opportunities for economic improvement in the home country, and in northern Albania especially.

Next, emigration has impacted strongly on Albanian demography. Quite apart from the loss of around one fifth of the country's population due to emigration between the censuses of 1989 and 2001, longer-term demographic effects should also be noted. One result of emigration can be detected in the annual statistics on births, which show a rapid decline since 1990.[84] At an aggregate level, emigration has abruptly halted the growth of the Albanian population. Throughout the period 1950-90, the Albanian population grew at 2-3 per cent per year (by 3.0 per cent during the 1950s, 2.7 per cent in the 1960s, 2.3 per cent in the 1970s and 2.0 per cent in the 1980s). During the 1990s (1989-2001) the population fell by 113,000 (-0.4 per cent per year), due to the massive net emigration, whereas birth and death parameters suggest that, with zero migration (as before 1990), the population should have grown by about 500,000 over the 1989-2001 intercensal period (or 1.3 per cent per year).

What is perhaps more worrying is the selectivity of the population loss. Comparison of the 1989 and 2001 population pyramids[85] reveals two 'holes' in the 2001 profile: young out-migrated adults aged 18-35 (especially marked on the male side of the pyramid); and an absence of young children – the 'unborn', due to mass emigration of young adults. Hence, emigration accelerates the ageing of the Albanian population: the proportion of the population aged less than 15 years fell from 33.0 to 29.3 per cent during 1989-2001, whilst those aged 65 or over rose from 5.3 to 7.5 per cent. An equally significant change has taken place within the working-age population: in 1989 the ratio of 15-34 year-olds to 35-64 year-olds was 1.5:1; by 2001 it had drastically fallen to 1:1.

Key social problems arising from age and gender selective out-migration are family separations and the abandonment of many older people. Our interviews contained many narrated examples of these issues, some of them included in chapter 3 of this report. Many wives and fiancées are separated from their emigrant husbands and partners. Children suffer too, from the absence of their fathers. But perhaps the most serious problem concerns older people who have lost their family and social support. Although Albanian custom obliges the youngest son and his wife to take care of his parents in their old age, this tradition is breaking down through emigration. Abandoned by their emigrant children and with declining social support and pensions in the new neo-liberal Albania, many older people, especially in isolated rural areas, are becoming 'orphan' pensioners.[86]

Albanian migration to the UK (and elsewhere) is a response to conditions of dire poverty which accompanied the abrupt exit from communism. Political chaos, insecurity and the re-emergence of blood feuds were additional factors for some migrants, along with limited professional and cultural horizons for the more educated. These factors have all helped to fuel substantial recent immigration of Albanians to the UK, especially to London and the surrounding region. Estimating the numbers involved would be pure guesswork. More important are their background characteristics (mainly young men from poor families originating in northern Albania), their clandestine arrival (mainly in the back of lorries), and their uncertain legal status (seeking asylum or undocumented). Because of their social background and their uncertain legal status in the UK, most Albanians are in a weak and vulnerable position in the labour market. They are confined to low-paid and insecure work in sectors such as construction and catering, often in the black economy. Over time some migrants improve their job status and pay as they become more established and gain a better grasp of English language and other skills.

Many families in Albania survive thanks to remittances sent by migrants working abroad. Particularly in rural areas, remittances are the main discriminator between poor and non-poor households. After satisfying basic needs, the main destination of remittances is the building of a new house or the expansion and improvement of an existing one. Prospects for return migration linked to the investment of migrant savings in improved farming and new businesses appear slight, due above all to the continuing economic, political and social climate in Albania. Most migrants in the UK are not contemplating returning, except for holiday and family visits. However, for migrants in a problematic legal situation, such return visits are practically impossible because of the difficulty of re-entry to the UK.

A viable policy framework

Before moving on to specific policy proposals, it is worth setting out their context and parameters. The starting point is that migration is a feature of our globalising world, and will continue to be so. As we have seen in the case of Albania, the pressures that drive the movement of people are immensely powerful and entrenched. It is unrealistic and self-defeating for the prosperous, industrialised countries to pursue a policy of preventing immigration: this will merely subvert it into irregular and increasingly illegal forms of entry and integration. By contrast, we contend that the development of systems of managed and facilitated migration are likely to prove to be of benefit to both sending and receiving countries, as well as migrants themselves.

- For migrants, such as the Albanians we interviewed, a managed migration system would offer the opportunity for legal migration channels, a chance to learn new skills and, for many, a route out of poverty. It is clear that irregular migrants currently pay large amounts in order to undertake highly risky journeys in the EU and UK. Once here, they risk exploitation in the irregular labour market, where many experience low wages and poor working conditions. For both these reasons there are strong incentives for migrants to use regular migration routes if they are available, so they can enter the country safely and more cheaply and access the adequate wages and safeguards of the regular labour market. Indeed, many migrants we interviewed expressed regularisation as a goal.

■ Managed and facilitated migration also offers advantages to the UK. As other studies have highlighted, immigration may be one of the key means by which the UK can address future demographic and economic problems created by an ageing population and a falling birth rate. Furthermore, evidence from this research demonstrates how policies of legal and managed migration into the UK may be the most constructive way of addressing the problem of irregular migration in its various forms. Managed migration also offers benefits to poor sending countries, in the form of remittances and the potential for the development of forms of personal and social capital in returning migrants.

■ For these reasons, our central recommendation is that the UK and EU should develop a viable and just system of managed migration, distinct from both the asylum system and existing measures for 'highly skilled' migrants. The UK Government has started to take constructive steps towards the introduction of a policy of managed immigration to the UK. In addition to the Highly Skilled Migrants Programme already in existence, the Chancellor announced in his Budget speech in April 2003, funding for measures designed to promote 'sector-based low-skilled migration' to the UK.

■ However, governments in affluent countries such as the UK must avoid treating immigrants solely as economic units of labour, and of implementing systems which are only designed to realise immediate economic benefits. It must be recognised that immigrant workers are also as human beings whose legal, political, economic, civil, social and cultural rights must be protected. It must also be recognised that migrant workers, whether regular or irregular, may be particularly vulnerable to abuse and exploitation in contravention of these rights. A viable and just system of managed migration must also protect the development interests of poor sending countries and in particular must go hand in hand with further economic development. Finally, managed immigration systems must recognise the economic pressures placed upon migrant workers, whose ability to send back remittances may be almost the sole survival strategy of his/her extended family, and must be set up to allow migrants to earn and send back remittances at an adequate level.

■ This approach to managed migration is clearly just, but it is also the best way to a viable migration policy. For a country such as the UK, policy interests in migration go beyond the remit of any one department, and certainly beyond the immediate labour market demand. There is a real need for coherent and co-ordinated policy response to migration (rather than simply immigration) which includes the priorities of the Foreign Office and Department for International Development, for example, as well as those of the Home Office and the Department for Work and Pensions. For this reason, our recommendations address not only issues around the management of entry and integration of economic/non-forced migrants to the UK and EU, but also those around social and economic development in poor sending countries, especially Albania. Indeed, specific recommendations are made to the Albanian Government.

Social and economic development
The EU and UK governments should reframe their migration policies to integrate social and economic development in migrants' home countries with entry and integration in host societies. By integrating development and migration policy, Western governments will reduce the longer-term pressure for migration, which in the case of Albania is overwhelmingly driven by extreme poverty and inadequate infrastructures. More immediately, an integrated approach will help to protect poor countries from the negative impacts of migration and thereby support the development programmes of the UK and EU. Indeed, the positive aspects of migration, not least remittances, can be harnessed to further such development.

According to the conclusions of the European Council dated May 19 2003 'the long-term objective of the community should be to continue to address the root causes of migration...in particular in poverty eradication, pro-poor economic growth, job creation, promotion of good governance, support for human rights.' [87] However, the conclusions of the June 22 2003 European Council meeting suggest that the priorities of European Union remain merely to establish greater security at international borders to reduce illegal migration, returns and migration monitoring, while largely ignoring the needs of people in poorer sending countries.

In the specific case of Albania, from 2002 to 2004, the EU has agreed to spend £49 million in Albania on border management, policing and judicial reform, but just £29 million on economic and social development in Albania.[88] This disparity in aid does little to help Albanians make a decent living from their land. Many choose instead to migrate to other countries. Therefore, the European Commission should review and make changes to its Country Strategy for Albania for 2002-2006, so that it reflects Albania's pressing development needs in the infrastructure, energy and agricultural sectors. In particular, greater emphasis needs to be given to the development of basic infrastructure such as electricity, water and roads and to developing access to education in poor rural communities, creating greater opportunities for employment, learning and social development. This has to be alongside support for the development of the physical and civil infrastructure, including strong norms of civil administration, reliable utilities and telecommunications.

Albanian development programmes, supported by international donors including the EU, should target impoverished communities in the mountainous area in northern Albania, a region that has recently received low levels of public assistance. Women in particular carry a large share of the burden when husbands and sons migrate abroad. Therefore, it is crucial that development programmes, which target impoverished communities, place a special emphasis on the needs of women. We have seen that, in the case of Albania, international migration is also closely linked to internal migration, particularly from the rural areas of the north to urban areas such as Tirana. The Albanian Government should therefore seek to reduce the pressures for internal migration and ensure that migrants have access to basic living conditions such as the provision of clean water, proper sanitation facilities and access to education.

Finally, migrants' financial and other capital needs to be harnessed better in furthering development in Albania. Remittances currently form a huge component of income, and yet appear to play a marginal part in social and economic development. To rectify this, the EU should support the Albanian Government to develop and implement legislation and programmes that would assist vulnerable communities to access credits and start new businesses. Similarly, the UK and EU should work with the Albanian Government to develop projects for the successful reintegration of returning migrants, which minimise potential friction and maximise the benefits of their skills and other social capital.

Entry

As already suggested, the UK should pursue a policy of managed economic migration for low-skilled workers, which creates a legal route of entry for low skilled economic migrants separate from other existing routes, such as asylum, family reunification or high-skill economic migration. This should build upon the steps which have already been initiated by the Government towards legal and managed migration for some low-skilled workers. Specifically, the current practice of permitting entry for five years, with the option of applying for settlement after four years, should be extended to low-skilled workers. This would allow migrants to enter for a period long enough to fulfil their personal needs and aspirations, and would recognise the contribution made by remittances to the survival of extended families and social development in the sending country – essential motivations for migration, particularly from Albania. Further, it would allow the migrant worker to earn sufficient amounts to make the initial investment in migrating worthwhile.

Entry should be structured by an asymmetric labour agreement between the EU and countries such as Albania. This could build upon the already established system of brokering association and co-operation agreements with third parties. Information about legal channels for migration and the rights of migrants in host countries should be available and accessible in urban and rural areas. Such a system would be important given the right of movement within the EU and – with the Albanian Government and international organisations – could be a means of providing would-be migrants with reliable information about regimes and opportunities within each country. It would also provide an alternative to irregular migration, help to assist with economic recovery and, in the specific case of Albania, increase the commitment of the EU to the integration process.

The EU 'gateway' should only be a preliminary stage through which applicants make their initial approach before dealing directly with their preferred destination countries. At this stage, entry criteria should be flexible enough to allow migrants to adjust to the prevailing labour market and social conditions within the UK, and for their personal migration projects to be realised. Account should be taken of the skills and competencies of would be migrants and should allow for workers from a range of labour sectors to work in the UK. Particular attention should be paid to opening up opportunities for women to gain work in the UK labour market, reflecting UK policy of promoting equal opportunities in employment.

Integration

Entry is only part of the policy context of managed migration. Equally important is the manner in which host countries manage the integration of newly arrived migrants. Even those coming to the UK for a relatively short period benefit from effective measures in this regard. Integration operates at three levels: first, by providing migrants themselves with the skills and information they need to operate in the UK; second, by using the law to enforce the rights of migrants and others; and finally, by ensuring that the climate of public opinion furthers good community relations.

As a matter of some priority, the UK Government should establish a comprehensive support and education system for migrants on arrival in the UK, aimed at educating migrants about the UK labour market, their legal rights and obligations as workers, advice and support on finding a job, how to access services, general social and cultural information about the UK, and English language teaching. This system should be available not only to workers themselves, but to their dependents, helping women who travel with their husbands/partners to develop their skills and find work themselves. The service would be mutually advantageous to potential employers and the UK economy, as well as to migrants themselves, as it would increase their skills and employability, and therefore their earning capacity, as well as helping workers to settle in UK society, access essential services, and avoid exploitation in the labour market. Such services should be free and take-up strongly encouraged. However, we do not recommend compulsory participation, not least as there is little reason to suppose that migrants would resist participation. On the contrary, a compulsory programme could be perceived as a method of policing migrants and consequently lead to resistance.

Integration will not be helped by the creation of a 'guest-worker' class who remain in the country for long periods of time, with no prospect of settlement or becoming full members of UK society. Subject to certain basic requirements (such as having no criminal record), migrant workers should be offered the opportunity of settlement in the UK within a reasonable period (the period currently operating in other UK migration schemes is four years)

The Government should address the problem of irregular workers currently in the UK by regularising their status with permission to work for one year. This would relieve the pressure that irregular migrant workers can create at the bottom end of the labour market. As irregular workers, employers can use such migrants to avoid employment protections, such as the National Minimum Wage; through regularisation, the rights of low-paid, vulnerable indigenous workers can better be protected. At the same time a highly exploitable, vulnerable group of workers themselves can be brought within the greater protections of the regular labour market.

Policing the irregular economy is a genuine issue for government. However, at present the risks of irregular employment are borne disproportionately by the – often migrant – workers, rather than the employer. Therefore, we recommend that measures to combat the informal economy should place a greater emphasis on employers who exploit migrant workers, rather than migrant workers themselves. This should include the establishment of an effective monitoring and complaints systems for migrant workers. The Government should work closely with trades unions to implement such a system.

The UK Government should ratify the UN Convention on the Rights of Migrant Workers and their Families, and take active steps to enforce the protection of these rights. The highly vulnerable status of migrant workers and their families demands special protection for this group, above and beyond existing legislation protecting the rights of all individuals in the UK such as the European Convention on Human Rights and the Human Rights Act. The UK Government has recognised the necessity of implementing special legislation to prevent discrimination against and protect the rights of other vulnerable groups. Migrant workers deserve similar legislative protections to ensure their rights to, for example, family reunification, and adequate access to welfare services.

If integration is to be successful, however, it needs to go beyond mechanistic programmes and legal rights. The indigenous community also needs to feel comfortable with a managed approach to migration. Certainly, the Government has a crucial role to play in shifting the terms of public debate around migration. Too much of the ground has been left to those who simply oppose immigration, often with a hint of racism, and the controversy around the asylum system indicates that there is a long way to go in convincing the public of the case for managed migration.

There has been a welcome attempt by the Government to set out the value of immigration to British society and economy, and this should be encouraged and extended. Similarly, the Government has been increasingly willing to challenge negative language from the press and other politicians, and this should be encouraged. Further, the Government should clearly define the terms used to describe migrants and to use these definitions in a clear and consistent manner, and should provide accurate information about labour migration into the UK, and the net contribution of migrant workers to the UK economy. This must be matched by a recognition that for some indigenous communities – often the most vulnerable – migration can present genuine pressures and competition for services and resources. The best way to address these concerns is not to deny them, but to improve the services and protections available to those communities.

But it is not only the Government that bears responsibility for reducing the hysteria that often surrounds this debate. Other politicians, public figures, and especially the press must look to their own behaviour. Some newspapers in particular have used crude language and stereotypes when dealing with the issue of immigration, and this has caused significant damage to community relations. Certainly an honest and open debate is needed, but this should not be based on prejudice and myths.

Finally, as an over-arching recommendation to the UK and Albanian Governments and the EU, we cannot stress too strongly the importance of establishing consultations with migrant workers and the organisations that represent them, as a way of ensuring that the voices of migrants can be heard in the debates around the development of migration policy and the key issues that concern them. The UK Government is already undertaking welcome explorations into ways of improving the participation of people living in poverty in the UK, and a similar approach should be taken towards migrant workers, who are so highly vulnerable and potentially marginalised. Only by hearing and learning from the experiences of migrant workers can systems be established that will protect their rights and help them to fulfil their legitimate aspirations.

References

1   *The Age of Migration*, S Castles and M Miller, Macmillan, 1998

2   *Secure Borders, Safe Haven: Integration with Diversity in Modern Britain*, Home Office, 2002

3   *Migration, Livelihoods and Rights: The Relevance of Migration in Development Policies*, A de Haan, Department for International Development, Social Development Working Paper 4, 2000

4   See for example *Workshop on the Migration and Development Nexus, Copenhagen, 15-16 April 2002, Mission Report*, European Commission, 2002. Also *Communication from the Commission to the Council, the European Parliament, the European Economic and Social Committee and the Committee of the Regions on Immigration, Integration and Employment*, Commission of the European Communities, COM (2003) 336 final, 3 June 2003

5   See Home Office Press Release 111/2003, 9 April 2003, 'Home Office announces Budget settlement'

6   'Blaming the victim: an analysis of press representation of refugees and asylum-seekers in the United Kingdom in the 1990s' by R Kaye in *Media and Migration: Constructions of Mobility and Difference*, R King and N Wood (eds), Routledge, 2001

7   *Immigration as an Economic Asset: The German Experience*, S Spencer (ed), IPPR/Trentham Books, 1994

        'An economic audit of contemporary immigration' by A Findlay in *Strangers and Citizens: A Positive Approach to Migrants and Refugees*, S Spencer (ed), IPPR/Rivers Oram Press, 1994

        Immigration, Development and the Labour Market, Paper for the International Conference on Migration Scenarios for the 21st Century, Rome, 12-14 July 2000) by I Visco

        Migration: an Economic and Social Analysis, Home Office, 2001

        The Migrant Population in the UK: Fiscal Effects, C Gott and K Johnston, Home Office, RDS Occasional Paper 77, 2002

8   It is true that some work has been done on Kosovar Albanians, but in this report we deal only with Albanians from the Republic of Albania

9   *International Migration Report 2002*, UN Department of Economic and Social Affairs, Population Division, 2002

10   *Trends in International Migration, Annual Report 2002*, OECD/SOPEMI, 2003.

11   *World Migration Report 2000*, International Organization for Migration and the United Nations, 2000

12   *ibid.*

13   *ibid.*

14   *ibid.*

15   *ibid.*

16   *ibid.*

17   According to the Status of the Office of the United Nations High Commissioner for Refugees adopted by General Assembly resolution 428 (V) of 14 December 1950, 'a refugee is a person who, owing to a well founded fear of persecution for reasons of race, religion, nationality or political opinion, is outside the country of his nationality and is unable or, owing to such fear, unwilling to avail himself of the protection of that country'

18   *World Migration Report 2000*, International Organization for Migration and the United Nations, 2000

19   'Key issues in international migration today' by G Hugo in *Migration at the Threshold of the Third Millennium*, Pontifical Council for the Pastoral Care of Migrants and Itinerant People, Vatican, 1998

20   'Migrant trafficking and smuggling in Europe: a review of the evidence' by J Salt and J Hogarth in *Migrant Trafficking and Human Smuggling in Europe,* International Organization for Migration, 2000. The statement is an over-simplification because people often have to engage the services of a smuggler/agent in order to flee persecution or other serious harm, which are violations of their human rights, because there is no 'legal' avenue open to them

21   Hugo *op. cit.*, Salt and Hogarth *op. cit.*

22   *World Migration Report 2000*, International Organization for Migration and the United Nations, 2000

23   Castles and Miller *op. cit.*, Hugo *op. cit.*

24   'Women in migration' by H Zlotnik in *Migration at the Threshold of the Third Millennium*, Pontifical Council for the Pastoral Care of Migrants and Itinerant People, Vatican, 1998

25   'Migration and globalization: a feminist perspective' by A Phizacklea in *The New Migration in Europe,* K Koser and H Lutz (eds), Macmillan, 1998

26   *The Global Migration Crisis*, Myron Weiner, Harper Collins, 1995

27   These figures are somewhat different from the UN series discussed previously since the EU data refer to officially-recorded foreigners, not foreign-born. Particularly in countries like France and Sweden, high rates of naturalisation make the 'foreign' population much lower than the 'foreign-born', whilst in countries like the UK and the Netherlands colonial history has given British or Dutch nationality to many foreign-born persons

28   *Caritas: Immigrazione Dossier Statistico 2001*, Anterem, 2001

29   In this regard, the picture will become clearer when the full results of Italy's most recent regularisation, completed in November 2002, are published. Most estimates of the total Albanian presence in Italy, including undocumented immigrants, suggest figures of around 200,000

30   For the latest data from the 1998 and 2001 Greek regularisations see 'Regularising the undocumented migrants in Greece: procedures and effects' by R Fakiolas, *Journal of Ethnic and Migration Studies*, 29(3), 2003

31   Estimating the total number of Albanians in Greece is also complicated by the large volume of 'shuttle migration' across the border - people who move to Greece for a few weeks or months to engage in short-term or seasonal work.

32   Of course, this 'televisual utopia' that the Italian TV channels presented to Albanians (and to Italians) was (and remains) a distorted view of reality. Above all it failed to acknowledge the exclusionary aspects of Italian society and hence to prepare Albanian migrants for the stigmatisation that they would soon be subject to. See 'Italy is beautiful: the role of Italian television in Albanian migration to Italy' by N Mai in *Media and Migration: Constructions of Mobility and Difference*, R King and N Wood (eds), Routledge, 2001 and 'Of myths and mirrors: interpretations of Albanian migration to Italy' by R King and N Mai in *Studi Emigrazione*, 145, 2002

33   On 29 March 1997, as a result of a collision between an Italian coastguard vessel and a boatful of Albanian migrants, 87 people, many of them women and children, lost their lives. According to one estimate, 340 Albanian would-be migrants were drowned or otherwise lost during 1999 alone. See *Albanian Human Development Report*, UNDP, 2000

34   'Contemporary patterns in Albanian migration' by K Barjaba, *South-East Europe Review*, 3(2), 2000

35   *The Population of Albania in 2001: Main Results of the Population and Housing Census*, INSTAT, 2002

36   'Globalization and migration: some pressing contradictions' by S Castles, *International Social Science Journal*, 50(2), 1998

37   'Globalization and human integration: we are all migrants' by J Nederveen Pieterse, *Futures*, 32(3), 2000

38   *The New Untouchables*, Nigel Harris, Penguin, 1996

39   *Economics and European Union Migration Policy*, Dan Corry, IPPR, 1996

40   'Migrants, institutions, politics: the evolution of European migration policies' by A Fielding in *Mass Migrations in Europe: the Legacy and the Future*, R King (ed), Belhaven Press, 1993 and 'International migration policies: 1950-2000' by R Appleyard, *International Migration*, 39(6), 2001

41   Fielding *op. cit.*

42   *The British Population,* D Coleman and J Salt, Oxford University Press, 1992

        Bordering on Control: A Comparison of Measures to Combat Irregular Migration in North America and Europe, P L Martin, International Organization for Migration, Research Paper 13, 2003

43   Fielding *op. cit.*

44   *Immigration and European Integration: Towards Fortress Europe?,* A Geddes, Manchester University Press, 2000

45   'Contextualising immigration policy implementation in Europe' by B Jordan, B Stråth and A Triandafyllidou in *Journal of Ethnic and Migration Studies,* 29(2), 2003

46   'International migration and state sovereignty in an integrating Europe' by A Geddes in *International Migration,* 39(6), 2001

47   *ibid.*

48   'New approaches to asylum?' by K Koser in *International Migration,* 39(6), 2001

49   The European Council on Refugees and Exiles

50   'International migration and state sovereignty in an integrating Europe' by A Geddes in *International Migration,* 39(6), 2001

51   Koser *op. cit.*

52   Martin *op. cit.*

53   This big cut was in line with many other EU countries (Austria 28 per cent, Belgium 20 per cent, Germany 11 per cent, Portugal 46 per cent) and with a 19 per cent decline in Europe as a whole. Sceptical journalists pointed out the special circumstances surrounding the UK figures - measured against a period (late 2002) when they were at an all-time high; and reflecting several specific events such as the closure of Sangatte, denial of cash benefits to those who fail to claim as soon as they arrive, restrictions on appeals etc. See 'Timing was key to asylum figures cut' by A Travis, *The Guardian,* 23 May 2003 and 'Blunkett's bogus asylum system' by S Naik, *Independent on Sunday,* 25 May 2003

54   'Welcome to camp Tirana' in *The Guardian,* 11 March 2003 and 'The Albanian solution' in *The Economist,* 15 March 2003. At the EU Summit in Thessaloniki in June 2003 Britain failed to win universal endorsement for the proposal, but gained limited approval for a pilot scheme, probably to be launched in East Africa for refugees fleeing continued war and famine in Somalia, and supported by Denmark, the Netherlands and Austria. See the EU Summit Report in *The Guardian,* 20 June 2003

55   This is the philosophical underpinning of a new programme of research which has just started at the Sussex Centre for Migration Research. Entitled 'Migration, Globalisation and Poverty' and funded by the UK Department for International Development as a 'Development Research Centre' for the five years starting June 2003, the new research programme will focus on four case-study countries: Albania, Bangladesh, Egypt and

Ghana. The Centre's director is Professor Richard Black. For further details see www.sussex.ac.uk/Units/SCMR.

56   *The Unsettled Relationship: Labor Migration and Economic Development,* D G Papademetriou and P L Martin (eds), Greenwood Press, 1991

57   'Interdependence between development and migration' by P A Fischer, R Martin and T Straubhaar in *International Migration, Immobility and Development,* T Hammar, G Brochmann, K Tamas and T Faist (eds), Berg, 1997

58   *The Migration of Labor,* O Stark, Blackwell, 1991

59   P Martin wrote about the migration hump largely in the context of Mexico-US migration. See for instance 'Economic integration and migration: the Mexico-US experience' in *International Migration into the 21st Century: Essays in Honour of Reginald Appleyard,* M.A.B. Siddique (ed.), Edward Elgar, 2001

60   For an excellent overview see *Migration and Chronic Poverty* (Chronic Poverty Research Centre, Working Paper 16), U Kothari, University of Manchester, 2002

61   There is an extensive literature on remittances; for some recent thinking see *Summary Report: Discussion on Migration and Development Using Remittances and Circular Migration as Drivers for Development,* K O'Neil, Migration Policy Institute and Center for Comparative Immigration Studies, University of California San Diego, Conference, 11-12 April 2003

62   *Harnessing the Potential of Migration and Return to Promote Development,* S Ammassari and R Black, International Organization for Migration, Research Paper 5, 2001

63   Barjaba *op. cit.*

64   *Emigracioni Ndërcombëtar dhe Familja - Lidhjet e Ndërsjellta,* V Misja and E Misja, MM, 1, 1995

65   Visco *op. cit.*

66   *Workshop on the Migration and Development Nexus, Copenhagen, 15-16 April 2002, Mission Report,* European Commission, 2002

67   *Poverty in Albania: A Qualitative Assessment,* H De Soto, P Gordon, I Gedeshi and Z Sinoimeri, World Bank Technical Paper 520, 2002

68   *ibid.* See also *A Fair Deal for Albanian Farmers,* Oxfam Briefing Paper 45, 2003.

69   *INSTAT: The Population of Albania in 2001, op. cit.*

70   *Human Development Report: Albania 2002,* UNDP, 2002

71   *Common Country Assessment: Albania,* Albanian Center for Economic Research, 2002

72   De Soto et al, *op. cit.*

73   *INSTAT: The Population of Albania in 2001, op. cit.*

74   *ibid.*

75   De Soto et al, *op. cit.*

76   *Human Development Report: Albania 2002*, UNDP, 2002

77   De Soto et al, *op. cit.*

78   Misja and Misja: *op. cit.*

79   *Migration for the Benefit of All: Towards a New Paradigm for Migrant Labor*, E Weinstein, International Labour Office, Immigration Papers 40, 2001

80   Barjaba *op. cit.*

81   De Soto et al, *op. cit.*

82   'From migrant to micro-entrepreneur: do-it-yourself development in Albania' by B Nicholson, *South-East Europe Review*, 4(3), 2001

83   *Oxfam: A Fair Deal for Albanian Farmers, op. cit.*

84   The yearly total for births remained remarkably steady at around 70,000 throughout the period between 1960 and the early 1980s, rising to 82,125 in 1990. Thereafter, dramatic changes occurred. Annual births fell during the first wave of emigration during the early 1990s (to 67,730 in 1993), rose again as temporary economic and political stability led to falling emigration during the mid-1990s (exceeding 70,000 births in both 1994 and 1995), and then fell again with the financial crisis of 1997 which provoked a fresh exodus (60,139 births in 1998). Annual births continued to fall during the late 1990s (to just 50,077 in 2000), probably due to a combination of factors - the long-term behavioural effect of a declining total fertility rate (from around 6 children per woman in the 1950s to 3.3 in 1990 and 2.2 in 2000), and the removal by emigration of many young adults, especially males, during part of their reproductive years.

85   *INSTAT: The Population of Albania in 2001, op. cit.*

86   De Soto et al, *op. cit.*

87   General Affairs and External Relations 2508th Council meeting, 9377/03, 19 May 2003 where the Council adopted the conclusions of the Communication from the Commission to the Council and the European Parliament: Integrating migration issues in the European Union's relations with third countries, 8927/03, 5 May 2003.

88   Albania: Country Strategy Paper 2002-2006 & Multi-Annual Indicative Programme (MIP) 2002-2004, European Community Cards Programme, 30 November 2001